how to start a home-based

Bakery Business

how to start a home-based

Bakery Business

Detra Denay Davis

Guilford, Connecticut

This book is dedicated to my daughter; I am proud to be your mother and in awe of the woman you have become. You are truly a pillar of wisdom, strength, and beauty.

To buy books in quantity for corporate use or incentives, call **(800) 962-0973** or e-mail **premiums@GlobePequot.com**.

Text design: Sheryl P. Kober
Layout artist: Kevin Mak
Project editor: Kristen Mellitt

Library of Congress Cataloging-in-Publication Data is available on file.

ISBN 978-0-7627-6082-4

Printed in the United States of America

10 9 8 7 6 5 4 3 2 1

Contents

01 So You Want to Start a Home-Based Bakery?

Never doubt that a small group of thoughtful, committed people can change the world. Indeed, it is the only thing that ever has.

—*Margaret Mead*

I recently read about a number of commercial bakers who were dead set against "cottage laws" that allow home-based baking. It is unknown if these baking professionals are afraid of the competition or just don't think there is enough business out here for both commercial establishments and home-based bakers. Personally I think there is room enough for everyone. There are those folks who do not want to purchase baked goods from commercial grocers, and there are others who will not purchase baked goods from anyone other than the long-established bakery on the corner.

I have always been a fan of purchasing homemade baked goods at local farmer's markets and farm stands. When I was growing up, neighbors sold their pecan pies, lemon pound cakes, and blackberry jams not only to make extra money but to share their delicious homemade goods with the community. These are memories seldom left to our children today with the upsurge of boxed cake mixes and the large-scale manufacturing of cookies and other baked goods.

For those who would argue that foods baked in the home put the public at risk, consider this: The risk is no greater than in a commercial bakery where employees occasionally come in to work even though they are ill. A home-based baker should and must operate using the same health safety rules and regulations as any other bakery business, particularly since home-based businesses carry the same liability as their commercial counterparts.

Still, there is a big difference between operating a traditional bakery and operating a home-based bakery, namely a number of home-based bakers want to specialize in just one thing, such as:

- Producing one special type of baked good
- Decorating cakes and/or cookies
- Baking just for family and friends

Anyone who wants to own a bakery has to start somewhere, and it is a good thing that states are beginning to recognize that not everyone is going to possess the revenue to start a traditional brick-and-mortar commercial bakery. Sometimes starting a small home-based baking business is the next best thing, if not the end goal in and of itself.

I started my first home-based baking venture after hearing about the American Pie Council's National Pie Day, part of a campaign to promote pie baking. The event is held every January 23, and since I absolutely love baking pies, I thought I would sell my signature creations at the local farmer's market that day. The whole venture did not get off to a great start, but little by little I got orders and sold a few pies here and there.

What I learned from this experience was that I really enjoyed learning about the business of home-based baking. The more I learned, the more I wanted to know. Starting a home-based bakery was not as simple as I initially anticipated, and not all baked goods are good candidates for a home-based baking business. I quickly learned to:

- Test my recipes and offer samples to get feedback.
- Set up delivery dates once or twice a month that only I knew about.
- Just do this when I wanted so it didn't become expensive or a burden.
- Create a select menu of pies (e.g., sweet potato, chocolate, pecan, apple, and cherry) that I wanted to bake, so I could change it up from time to time. Use pie boxes with windows on them.
- Use store-bought or my own homemade pie crust. (If homemade, I always purchased my own aluminum pie tins. Purchasing your own tins allows you to determine the size and depth of the pie you make, while store-bought crust can limit those choices.)
- Stock my pantry with other supplies/ingredients so I have the products needed to prepare a pie should I receive unexpected pie orders.

- Perform a trial delivery run to see how things go.
- Give out samples of tested recipes to potential customers. It is great, as mentioned, to allow family and friends to test your recipes prior to offering them for sale. Avoid selling products that have not been tested; the more input from taste testers the better.
- Pay close attention to what works and what doesn't.

Dropping off pies throughout the community and building a buzz was a great way to give folks the opportunity to taste my signature baked goods. However, looking back I learned a number of things about selling; namely don't assume everyone is going to want or need what you have to offer. If your friends say "You really should sell that German chocolate pie, it's heavenly" take that advice with a grain of salt, it does not mean you should do it. Do your homework: A bit of market research on the most popular flavor trends for your product line will help you understand what your customers want.

Before I spent money on a Web domain name and hosting, I created a blog and started telling my community about my pies. "If you bake it they will come" may or may not be true. Building a buzz, a following, a stream of food fans is imperative.

Assessing Your Skills and Resources

I can't count all of the people I have run across in my life who have had unbelievably innovative food ideas yet who fell into a hole because they did not have the tenacity or faith to follow their dream or a solid plan to take them where they wanted to go. It might not be an earth-shattering, one-of-a-kind product; it might be taking something ordinary like cake balls and decorating them to perfection or making circular brownies as opposed to brownie squares. Whatever your product, the real challenge is taking that first leap of faith after doing a substantial amount of homework. You take a simple idea, something you like, something you have a passion for, and turn it into a unique product, a product that is not on the market or one that is better than anything else on the market.

Before you dive into your new venture, take a few minutes to take stock of your current situation. You may not be able to answer all of the following questions now; however, after reading the book and investigating your local, state, and federal requirements, you should be able to answer all of them:

- What is your reason for starting a home-based bakery business?

- What impact will a home-based business have on your family life?

- Do you have the necessary capital to fund this new business?

- What are your strengths?

- What are your weaknesses?

- Will you need additional outside help to produce your baked goods?

- What is your product?

- What is the name of your product?

- Where will you make your product—at home or in a kitchen incubator? A kitchen incubator is a business incubator dedicated to helping food entrepreneurs in the early stage of a catering, retail, or wholesale food business.
- What local, state, and federal regulations apply that will enable you to bake from home legally and profitably?

Home-based bakers work long, odd hours. Some bakers begin work around 2 or 3 a.m. and end work around noon, so they have time to deliver their product and address the needs of their family. For many bakers the talent associated with baking and cake decorating is often innate, and baking is one of the last job areas where talent may outweigh education. Home-based baking is not without its disadvantages however. It is a physically demanding; you're standing on your feet and moving around the kitchen, all while addressing phone calls from customers and e-mailing customers about the details of their orders. You'll need stamina, focus, and skill, so assess your weaknesses and strengths carefully.

Business Basics 101

The operation surrounding a home-based bakery is relatively simple and selling baked goods to the public involves a few fundamental practices. It is important to keep your product and service selection small since you are operating from your residence and may not have room to maintain product supplies and storage.

Understand the core of your bakery business and keep it simple. Knowing the costs and margins for each product will allow you to determine its profitability.

Select five or so areas that are critical to the success of your home-based bakery. It is important to know how to track and assess your success no matter what type of business you operate. Creating benchmarks that outline where you should be as you develop your home-based bakery will ensure you are meeting your business development goals and objectives.

For example, five areas critical to your success may include:

1. Selecting a product that can be produced throughout the seasons and will not suffer when the weather is excessively warm or cold
2. Selecting a product that is affordable to make, yet not too expensive to the consumer
3. Selecting packaging that is biodegradable and not harmful to the environment
4. Securing a selling location that is close to your home so transporting the product is never an issue
5. Selecting payment plans that allow customers to pay by credit

A home-based baker bakes and sells breads, cakes, and other baked goods like cookies, pies, biscotti, petit fours, and pastries. One advantage of being a home-based bakery is the ability to bake from the comfort of home all while making extra income; and although products produced are often sold to neighbors, community members, at food co-ops, farmer's markets, flea markets, and to local vendors, some bakers elect to have private customers that purchase directly from the baker's Web site.

The concept of home-based baking is hardly new; in fact during the Middle ages, it was common for each landlord to have a bakery, which was actually more of a public oven. Housewives would bring dough that they had prepared to the baker, who would use the oven to bake it into bread. As time went on, bakers began to bake their own goods, creating numerous tricks of the trade. For example, some bakers had trap doors that would allow a small boy to pinch off a bit of the dough to later sell as his own. This practice eventually led to a regulation known as the "Assize of Bread and Ale,"[1] which provided harsh punishments for bakers who were caught cheating their customers. In response, bakers commonly threw in an extra loaf of bread; this tradition lives on today and is known as the "baker's dozen."

---

1 Ross, Alan S.C., The Assize of Bread, The Economic History Review, Vol. 9, Issue 2, Pages 332 - 342, 1956.

Small Independent bakeries—aka home bakeries—are largely family-run businesses. They may specialize in particular types of products, such as sourdough or Artisan breads, Danish pastry, butter cakes, home-made cookies, and bars and today more bakers are becoming interested in preparing organic products and products that are wheat, gluten, dairy, and sugar free.

As you start to think about the development of your home-based bakery, ask yourself the following questions:

What are your thoughts about a home-based bakery?

Even though you are at home, you are still operating a business from your home and there is an enormous amount of responsibility associated with serving the public in a private dwelling. Can you handle mixing business and family?

What is the goal of your home-based bakery?

Are you starting a bakery in hopes of one day moving into a brick-and-mortar location or are you simply operating your business to make extra income? Perhaps you have another reason?

What is unique about your product?

Everyone wants to think they have a unique product, but have you compared your products to competitors? If you could list three things that make your baked goods stand out from the status quo, what would it be?

How would you define your home-based bakery?

Think about how you will operate this business. Many home-based bakers like to select their baking days and not bake to order, while others will bake when an order is received via email or phone order. Think about what will work best for your business based on the type of product you prepare. There are times when you cannot bake a product on demand. Is this something you are willing to do?

What hours of operation will you have? Will you deliver?

Operating a home-based bakery does not mean you are baking 24/7. You are at home and your family will expect you to provide for their needs even if you are baking a cake for a customer. Will you be able to deliver the cakes when the kids are in the back seat of your car? Think carefully about how you will structure the operational aspects of your home-based bakery so it is effective and efficient.

How will you package your product?

Many home-based bakers live in areas that do not offer the supplies and packaging for their products and must purchase items online. Is this something you are willing to do? There are also customers who are expecting their products to be packaged in environmentally safe packaging. How would that impact the vision you have for you home-based bakery? Do you want to use only "green" products and how accessible are they to you?

Will you sell in bulk or as individual products?

Consumers have enough temptations and don't need huge coffee cakes or traditional 9-inch or 10-inch cakes and pies to distract them from eating in moderation and controlling those sweet cravings. Would you be willing to consider offering pint-size products individually packaged? How will that impact your bottom line?

Are you a wholesaler or a retail establishment?

Making the decision to sell your products retail or wholesale should not be taken lightly. Direct sales is popular with most home-based bakers, however those who rent licensed commercial kitchen facilities often sell wholesale because they can produce more product and sell in bulk.

Who are your customers?

Determining your customer base is instrumental to the success of your products and your business. Are you in a community where gluten-free baked goods are in demand and no one is addressing the issue? Is this something you might learn more about and supply the demand?

Are you willing to enter into a contract to supply your products?

Your home-based baking business can be as large or small as you want it depending on who you will service. It is sometime easier to control direct sales than contracting with a vendor and supplying bulk products, where the amount needed can fluctuate from week to week.

Home-Based Baking Rules and Regulations

The rules and regulations surrounding the operation of a home-based bakery are different in every state and sometimes in every county. Before starting your home bakery business you may need to fulfill a number of requirements. For example, your water source must be a safe source that is used, transported, and dispensed in a sanitary manner. You may be prevented from operating a home-based bakery if you live in a mobile home or if you have pets. Either the local health department or the state department of agriculture is the authority that will inspect your home/kitchen incubator to ensure it is clean and ready to produce wholesome, delicious cakes, pies, cookies, breads, and pastries for public consumption. Some type of license or permit is usually required to operate a home-based bakery or small food processing operation and you will need to procure an additional business license from the local, county, or state licensing agency.

Some regulatory agencies require that each and every recipe for each individual product be reviewed by a food processing authority, so check with your regulatory agency or compliance officer. You also may need to develop a standard recipe with exact quantities (in grams of weight, not volume) and exact temperatures and times for processing. When this has been completed, you may be asked to send or take a sample of your product, the recipe with exact ingredients, and your process, noting times and temperatures, to your compliance agency. The food product should be submitted in the container in which you wish to sell it.

Some regulatory agencies provide testing that evaluates the pH for pickled foods and salsa, water activity for baked and canned foods, acidity for vinegars, Brix for jams, jellies, and syrups, and water phase salt for smoked seafood. These tests will determine if your food product falls under proper guidelines for food safety or standards of identity for the U.S. Food and Drug Administration (FDA). If the food does not meet these guidelines, your compliance officer can suggest improvements or ask that your products be prepared in a licensed commercial kitchen facility.

Food producers who sell directly to the public and make no more than $50,000 per year are exempt from adding a nutrition label. However, if you would like to add that label to your product, you may wish to speak with your local compliance officer. In the state of North Carolina, for instance, the Department of Agriculture and Consumer Services is available to assist; however there may be some cost for those services.

An Organized Bakery Business

Starting a home-based bakery means you are about to begin a challenge unlike any other. There are complications and decisions that will need to be made, along with responsibilities that involve sometimes setting aside your needs and the needs of your family. Developing good organizational skills can and will help you develop a business that functions like a well-oiled machine.

I have met a number of home-based bakers who have suffered from not organizing their home bakeries and the paperwork affiliated with operating them. The first thing that getting organized can do for you is assist you in tracking your income, expenditures, taxes, and inventory. I often tell my students that starting a home-based bakery is a lot like planning for multiple births. At any given time, you will be responsible for and expected to feed a number of customers; the only difference is that you really don't know when they are going to show up.

All home-based bakers must possess organizational systems if they are to eliminate much of the confusion from their daily operations. You must constantly think about the supplies you need to run your business, the ingredients needed to prepare every product you want to sell, and the labels and packaging you will need in order to set your product apart from your competitors.

Organization doesn't just happen; it is something you must address daily and work to keep in place. It can begin with a simple "to do" list and turn into a weekly calendar of business routines. If you are not familiar with how to get organized, the Internet is a fantastic source of information that can assist you in structuring your daily responsibilities. Organizing your business can and will save you both time and money, and your customers and suppliers will appreciate it in the long run.

How to Use This Book

Home-based baking is a rewarding and interesting business, and it allows bakers to exhibit their creativity and their love for the craft of baking. What could be better than making delicious baked goods for the people in your community and even introducing them to new flavors and custom products? It is the goal of this book to provide you with the basic information needed to start your home-based bakery business. The journey may be challenging, particularly if you live in a location that does not allow you to operate from your home kitchen. When you read the interviews from other home-based bakers that appear at the end of the book, you will soon realize that nothing is impossible.

Helpful Web Sites

The following Web sites will assist you in not only getting your home-based bakery off to a great start, but in organizing your bookkeeping and accounts, pricing your goods, and working with wholesale distributors.

http://dwmbeancounter.com

This site provides free interactive online bookkeeping and accounting tutorials and courses. If you have no experience in small business bookkeeping and accounting, this is the place to start.

www.komida.com

This account management system is designed specifically for small specialty food companies. It works with the accounting system you currently use and allows you to take your wholesale business to the next level.

http://quickbooks.intuit.com/

Quickbooks is a bookkeeping program that requires no accounting experience. The program provides a simple, online guided tour so you will quickly become familiar with drafting checks and creating invoices, along with tracking sales, expenses, and tax information. There are online tutorials and free technical support.

www.inc.com/tools

Tools from INC.com is a library of sample small business tools, templates, worksheets, and spreadsheets for small business owners.

www.cakeboss.com/

The Cake Boss is a software program that will assist the home-based baker with calculating the exact cost of making a cake, including hourly labor cost. The program tracks expenses, prints invoices, and is invaluable to the cake baker.

Go through each chapter and plan your home-based bakery carefully. Since you will be working from home, you want to organize your bakery in such a way that it puts as little stress on the family unit as possible. Starting a home-based bakery does not allow you the luxury of ignoring runny noses and lost homework. Very often home-based bakers are one-person operations, and it can get lonely; but there are chapters in the book that will walk you through how to schedule your time and design your day in such a way that you are not only caring for your family and your customers but also yourself.

Enjoy the journey, and I wish each and every one of you the very best in your new baking career!

02 | Setting Up Your Home Bakery Business

A home-based bakery business can operate as a full- or part-time venture. How much time you commit to the bakery is dependent on how often you want to bake your products. Most home bakers are attracted to a home-based bakery business because it offers flexibility concerning their time and the opportunity to showcase and sell their favorite baked goods.

During the planning stage, you will need to organize your kitchen and set aside a separate space for completing paperwork, making and returning phone calls, and printing labels for your baked goods. Like any small business owner, you will be responsible for all the grunt work unless family members or close friends are willing to assist you.

Starting a home-based business often involves more work than originally anticipated, but once you organize your business and decide what you will sell, you can focus on developing your bakery and promoting your products. Let's take a look at seven basic steps you might take to initiate the home-based bakery start-up process:

Step 1: Think about what type of product your community not only wants but needs. Pay attention to what is missing in the marketplace. Have you heard of anyone complaining about a lack of gluten-free baked goods or sugar-free cookies? Is there a new product idea that could fill this need?

Step 2: Do research in your community to find out if your new product idea has been tried. If it has, go back to Step 1 and search for another new product idea; for example if you want to do a cookie with orange and pecans, consider producing a biscotti or scone using the same ingredients.

Step 3: When you have a solid new product idea, create a recipe that produces a superior product, and once the product is perfected, mum's the word.

Step 4: Now it's time to create a sample product and offer it for free to the public. You may also want to design special packaging and a label.

Step 5: Test your new product and have family, friends, and the general public evaluate it in its entirety (e.g., flavor, texture, color, taste, etc.). Make sure you state any allergens that may be in the product, such as dairy, nuts, etc. (See Chapter 2— Basic Pantry Items, Package and Label Requirements. The Food and Drug Administration Food Allergen Labeling and Consumer Protection Act of 2004. 21 USC 301. provides additional information about allergens and is available online at www.fda.gov/Food/LabelingNutrition/FoodAllergensLabeling/GuidanceComplianceRegulatoryInformation/ucm106187.htm .

Step 6: After you've properly designed and tested your new product, it's time to start the marketing process and decide how you will take your product from kitchen to market.

Step 7: Take time to assess what your start-up cost will be for operating a home-based bakery. This is the point where you will need to examine how many different products you will sell and the cost associated with each product. The more products you produce, the more ingredients you will need to have on hand. When first starting out it is best to sell one or two products and build a buzz.

Setting Up Your Kitchen

Working out of your home kitchen can prove to be challenging. It is imperative that you organize your kitchen in such a manner that the utensils and food production equipment you use for your family are separate from that used for the production of the baked goods you sell to the public.

If you live in a state that allows you to bake from home and sell to the public, the regulatory agency that oversees your food production may ask that you separate cooking and baking utensils used for your business. If that is the case, simply store your bakery supplies in a separate pantry or cupboard and ask family members not to use anything in those designated cupboards.

Start-up Costs Worksheet

Basic baking equipment and supplies	$
Initial cost of baking ingredients	$
Business license	$
Bakery tax (if applicable)	$
Attorney and accounting fees	$
Rental fees for selling locations (farmer's markets, community fair stands, etc.)	$
Insurance	$
Office supplies	$
Telephone and Internet access	$
Taxes	$
Rainy day fund	$
Miscellaneous expenses based on your specific home-based baking needs	$

In most cases you will not need to use a separate stove/oven and refrigerator. In some states you are not allowed to bake from home and sell your products (check with your state department of agriculture or local health department), so you will need to rent a licensed commercial kitchen (or kitchen incubator) and prepare your products in a commercial facility. Often such facilities may provide all the necessary cooking and baking equipment you will need to produce your baked goods.

If you must work with a kitchen incubator, the facility owners will supply you with all the information you will need to produce your product. They may ask you to complete an application process, provide proof of liability insurance, and commit to using the facility for a specified period of time. It is important to ask questions and understand your responsibilities before making a commitment to work with an incubator or shared kitchen facility. Many of these facilities are not government-sponsored and are in business to not only help small food processors but to make money themselves. You can find kitchen incubator listings online. Key Web sites include:

1. Commercial Kitchens for Rent—www.commercialkitchenforrent.com
2. Culinary Incubator—www.culinaryincubator.com/maps.php
3. Find-An-Incubator Kitchen—http://homebasedbaking.com/ find-an-incubator-kitchen

When storing the ingredients for your home-based bakery products, keep all ingredients separate from those items you use every day for your family. This will help you oversee the ingredients inventory used in the production of your baked goods and assure that you are using the freshest products first and rotating your ingredients accordingly.

You may be tempted to use your bakery business products when you run out of ingredients for home use, but avoid doing that if at all possible. Think of your home-based bakery as a facility apart from your home; there is nothing worse than running out of ingredients for a product being made for a paying customer; plus, you may not always have time to run out and purchase ingredients when you have a delivery deadline fast approaching.

Organizing your product ingredients and equipment will also assist you in organizing the operational flow of your production process. Take time to examine how you will utilize your time and space; for example if you are baking six pies in your double ovens, you will need to perform a walk-through to see what is needed to produce the pie crust, fill the pie tins, bake the pies, and lay them on racks to cool. Ask yourself, "Will I have enough space in the kitchen? Will I need to place the pies on the dining room table to cool, and where will I box and label the finished products?"

Your home-based bakery operation should run like a well-oiled machine, and if you find yourself frustrated because you can't locate ingredients, equipment, or packing supplies, you will want to rethink the operational process you have assigned to the setup of your home-based bakery until you get it right.

Family Helpers in the Kitchen

One of the advantages of operating a home-based bakery is the flexibility it offers you in relation to time with your family. There are some home-based bakers who allow their older children to assist in the food preparation, while others choose to bake while their children are at school. How you set up your baking responsibilities depends on your and your family's needs.

If you are going to allow your children to assist you in this business venture, a certain degree of caution should be taken. You do not want children exposed to hazardous conditions, such as using sharp objects like knives and other sharp cutting tools. You also do not want your children to participate in any activity that will potentially ruin a product that is being sold to one of your customers.

It is imperative that you teach your children basic food safety skills and explain that, although this is the family kitchen, it is also your workplace, and there are things they will not be able to do during the time you are preparing baked goods for customers.

You will want to remember that running in and out of the kitchen during prep time increases the chances for accidents; and opening and closing the refrigerator door reduces the temperature in the refrigerator, putting the food stored there at risk. So consider placing family snacks and drinks in a common area of your home where your children can "grab and go" and you can maintain control over the kitchen area.

Here are some recommendations for keeping your kitchen safe:

- Use trays and carts to carry multiple items
- Post proper hand-washing precautions (see sidebar)
- Remove trash bins from the direct work area
- Dispose of oil waste properly
- Wear heat-resistant gloves or mitts when handling hot utensils and removing baked goods from the oven
- Wear nonslip footwear, preferably with rubber soles
- Make sure ventilation and/or air-conditioning systems work well
- Use a floor cleaning product that effectively removes oil and grease
- Clean up spills immediately to prevent any slipping accidents
- Make sure the exit from the kitchen is unobstructed
- Clear clutter from passageways and work areas
- Ensure that there is adequate lighting
- Post signs to warn of hot equipment and pans
- Store towels, curtains, and other flammables away from the range
- Wear clothing with short or close-fitting sleeves while baking
- Mount a fire extinguisher, fully visible and unobstructed, near an exit

Prior to starting your home-based bakery, visit http://homebasedbaking.com/knowledgebase/cottage-laws to view the cottage food laws for your state. Cottage food laws are state and county regulations governing residents baking from home for profit. If your state is not listed on the Web site you will need to contact your state Department of Health or your state Department of Agriculture to learn about

Handwashing Guidelines

The following guidelines are based on information found on the Center for Disease Control's (CDC) website, www.cdc.gov.

1) Wet your hands under warm, running water. Avoid contact with the faucet after this point.
2) Lather the soap on your hands for at least ten to fifteen seconds and then rub your hands together vigorously.
3) Wash your palms, in between your fingers, under your fingernails, and the back of your hand; focus on the ends of your fingers.
4) Rinse your hands thoroughly under the warm running water.
5) Dry your hands with a clean towel or paper towel from a receptacle.
6) Turn off the water using the towel to turn the nozzle. This will help to keep your hand from being contaminated again. By following the above steps, decontamination is assured. The entire process should take no longer than a minute and can be done in pretty much any sink.

food processing regulations. The regulatory agency that issues the license or permit for you to operate your home-based bakery may provide additional safety precautions for you follow. You can also take the initiative and ask them if they have other suggestions for keeping your kitchen safe.

Complying with Government Requirements

Several types of commercial food processing in the home kitchen are typically permitted by local health departments and state departments of agriculture. Unfortunately every municipality and state government has its own rules and regulations. It is the responsibility of each home-based baker to abide by the policies set by the regulatory agency with jurisdiction over the kitchen. If you are not sure whether home-based food processing is allowed in your state, contact your state department of agriculture or local health department. Food sales allowed under department of agriculture regulations are usually limited to state-sponsored farmer's markets; you must contact your regulatory agency to learn if there are any exemptions.

The types of foods legally prepared in home kitchens are often limited to foods that are not "potentially hazardous." Foods that are potentially hazardous are those that can support a group of pathogenic microorganisms and that require strict temperature controls. All potentially hazardous food must be produced in a commercially licensed/registered kitchen.

This general rule does not specifically prohibit home processing of potentially hazardous foods because the foods may be produced in a second kitchen, meeting all regulatory standards separate from the private home kitchen; but this can only be determined by your local regulatory agency.

The most common types of food produced in home kitchens include but are not limited to bakery products (cakes, cookies, breads), jams, jellies, acidified foods, and some candies; and each type of food processing may have certain requirements and limitations, so it is imperative that every home-based baker contact the appropriate regulatory agency for all product requirements.

General rules for producing food products in your home kitchen may include but are not limited to the following:

- No animals/pets are permitted in the home at any time.
- Home-based baking may be limited to those owning farms or growing their own produce.
- In some states it is recommended that children not be in the kitchen area during commercial processing; if you are unsure, contact your state regulatory agency to learn about food processing restrictions.
- The water supply serving the home must be from an approved supply. Private sources such as well water must be tested annually for various forms of bacteria.
- Home-based baking regulatory approval cannot be in conflict with any local zoning or ordinances. In some instances a written statement from the local municipality must be obtained.
- Registration and fees may be required by some regulatory agencies.
- All ingredients must be separate from those for personal use and must be properly stored and protected.
- There may be restricted use of the home kitchen during any commercial processing.

- Products for sale must be properly labeled in accordance with state and local regulatory guidelines, which may include but not be limited to: name of product, name and address of manufacturer, ingredients listed in decreasing order by weight, net weight, or unit count, and allergens in the product (dairy, nuts, etc.).
- Nutritional labeling may be required on food products being shipped and/or sold in interstate commerce. (Some home businesses may qualify for a small business exemption from the nutritional labeling requirement by appealing to the Food and Drug Administration.)
- Regulatory agencies may limit the amount of product sales a home-based baker may gross every year.
- Home-based bakers may be required to carry liability insurance when selling home-processed foods to the public.
- Home-based bakers may be asked to demonstrate knowledge of the state and/or local food code as it applies to their specific operations.
- A three-compartment sink or a commercial-style dishwasher may be required for dishware-washing.
- Home-based bakers may be required to use separate drain boards for soiled and clean dishes.
- Home-based bakers may be asked to use "approved sanitizers" for food contact surfaces and test kits to check for contamination.
- Home-based bakers may be asked to place a shield over and around light fixtures to prevent breakage.
- All hood systems over the range should be adequately vented.
- Thermometers may need to be placed in refrigerators and freezers to monitor the temperatures.

It should be noted that the suggestions above are implemented to prevent foodborne illness and to maintain a safe, secure food-processing environment for you and your customers.

Renting a Kitchen Incubator

A kitchen incubator is a fully licensed commercial kitchen, and its primary purpose is to help food entrepreneurs expand their business and prepare and/or process products at reasonable rental rates, allowing the user to select the amount of time needed to prepare food products.

Depending on the needs of the user, the kitchen incubator can make available various types of equipment, e.g., ovens, ranges, refrigerators, freezers, mixers, food processors, work tables, kitchen utensils, and cold storage space. Some incubators even provide a wide range of training, support services, and resources connecting entrepreneurs with business development centers. Keep in mind that the variety of services provided by kitchen incubators will vary, and the more services you receive, the more you may have to pay.

Kitchen incubators, or *shared kitchens* as they are sometimes called, also serve as culinary workshops where food innovators can create their food products and learn to grow their business. It is the location where a food entrepreneur can learn to move his or her products from the home kitchen to the open market.

Kitchen incubators and shared kitchen facilities offer perhaps the best alternative food-production locations for home-based bakers. Each kitchen incubator or shared kitchen is operated differently, and there is usually a fee associated with its use. A kitchen incubator allows home food processors the opportunity to test-market their products before renting a commercial building or investing in a commercial distribution process.

The kitchen incubator may not fit every baker's needs, since it may not be worth traveling to the site to produce products if the location is several miles away. However, if a processor needs to make 20 to 30 cheesecakes in four to five hours, having tons of space for dry and cold food storage, baking equipment, and a shared office may make the use of such a facility beneficial.

Some kitchen incubators are also business incubators committed to assisting food entrepreneurs in the early stages of their product development and distribution. Kitchen incubators are often located in rural areas; however, recently there has been an influx of kitchen incubators popping up in urban areas, too. It is the goal of a kitchen incubator to circumvent the high cost of an investment involved in renting a commercial space or the purchase of commercial equipment along with the high liability associated with operating a brick-and-mortar food-processing facility.

Often kitchen tenants using incubators or shared kitchen rentals will need to be approved by a selection committee composed of members of the incubator center, and the tenants may be asked to pay an amount that covers the expenses, upkeep, and maintenance of the facility. It is imperative that home-based bakers who must

Kitchen Incubator Checklist

There are many states where home-based bakers and small food processors are not allowed to prepare food in their home kitchen. If you must use a kitchen incubator or shared kitchen facility, there are a few things you will need to know to protect your new business venture.

- Make sure before completing an application that the kitchen incubator or shared-kitchen facility is licensed and insured. It should provide a safe, clean environment for food preparation.

- Inspect the facility thoroughly to make sure it has all the equipment and supplies you will need to prepare your product.

- Ensure that ample storage and lockers are available.

- Ask the administrators of the facility if there are other services, such as Internet and phone use, or business advice they offer, or if you are only paying for the use of the kitchen.

- Require a signed contract to secure the use of the facility for a specified length of time and amount of money. You will need to provide your own ingredients, small appliances, cooking and baking utensils, cleaning supplies, and other products needed to operate your business unless otherwise mentioned in the contract.

Some incubator or shared kitchen facilities may require the following from you:

- Completion of an application

- References

- A business license

- Liability insurance that names the incubator facility as "additionally insured"

- Caterer's license or food handler's license

- Food handler's certificate

- Security/cleaning deposit

Below is a checklist that will assist you in selecting the best facility for product preparation.

Question	Yes	No	Comment
Does the kitchen incubator or shared use facility require the completion of an application for use?			
Does the facility require you to fill out and return a User Contract that includes rental and use of equipment policies?			
Does the facility require you attend any type of Food Safety and Sanitation workshop or provide proof of similar type training?			
Does the facility schedule a specific time you can use the kitchen and is that time set or does it vary? (Offering flexibility allows bakers to use the facility when they have product to produce, saving time and money.)			
Does the facility require the baker to prepay for scheduled use of the kitchen and/or pay a security deposit to secure use of the rented kitchen?			
Does the facility require the baker to complete an Emergency Contact Form in the event of an accident?			

use these facilities weigh whether participating in these organizations is worth the money, time, and effort. Like any other business, incubators are also in business to make money.

Potential incubator tenants may be required to submit business, financial, and marketing plans offering a road map of how they will start and grow their business. In addition there are other variables that need to be addressed, such as whether products will need to be refrigerated and stored or packaged for shipping at the incubator location, and whether vendors are allowed to pick up products directly from the kitchen incubator location. The average tenant will have a limited time to participate in the use of the incubator's facility. The amount of time typically allowed to use such a facility is between twelve and thirty-six months. Presumably this is enough time for the tenant to move his or her business from the incubator stage to a full-fledged, freestanding business.

Your community may or may not have an incubator or shared kitchen facility. Many bakers ask churches with commercial kitchens, diners, and small restaurant owners if they can use their commercial facilities; however, there may be an issue with who is liable if there is a mishap at the facility. Most incubators are designed to take that risk, thereby providing start-up bakers with a viable place to get started.

Equipping Your Kitchen

Every piece of equipment in your kitchen should answer one fundamental question: Does it help you prepare your goods? You don't need every gadget in those overly stocked bed and bath stores, and you don't need high-end mixers and food processors. If you do some comparison shopping and remember that the most expensive items are not always the best, you will end up stocking your kitchen with equipment that is not only functional but also affordable.

How to Select a Food Processor

A food processor is the most versatile small appliance when it comes to chopping, grinding, mixing, and pureeing foods. Like blenders, they are an essential piece of equipment for even the novice baker. Food processors save time and eliminate waste. When looking for the ideal food processor, there are a number of things to consider:

- Models that feature work bowls made from shatterproof material.
- Models with a sturdy base.

- Mini-prep processors are ideal for preparing small amounts of food.
- Large processors should have wide feeding tubes and covered work bowls with handles.
- Large models should be equipped with not only stainless steel blades but also slicing and shredding discs.
- The best models will have sturdy die-cast metal housings and powerful induction motors.
- Remember to select models with a warranty, and make sure the manufacturer offers replacements on blades and other attachments.

The price of a food processor will depend on its size and the accessories that come with it. If you don't need the bells and whistles, don't buy them. Mini processors may be purchased for less than $60, but the workhorse models list for $400 or more.

How to Select a Kitchen Mixer

Having the right tools is over half the battle when it comes to preparing your favorite baked goods, and although blenders are great for mixing small amounts of ingredients, particularly liquid ingredients, most home-based bakers will need a heavy duty mixer at some point if they are preparing large quantities of their products.

There are several things to consider when purchasing a mixer, beginning with knowing what type of baked goods you will prepare. If your main prep focuses on simple brownie, cake, or cookie recipes, a standard quality hand mixer will suffice. The preparation of more complex foods, such as homemade breads, complicated recipes, or thick batters (e.g., pound cake) may involve purchasing a mixer with a stand. These mixers are more powerful than a handheld mixer and will work by themselves, allowing a baker to work on another part of the recipe.

Today many stand mixers have attachments, such as pasta rollers, meat grinders, and ice cream makers. If you don't need it, don't get it. There is nothing worse than having all these little attachments in the bottom of a drawer collecting dust. As your baking business advances, there will be plenty of time to purchase bells and whistles.

Another consideration is space and storage. Do you want these small appliances to sit on a counter or in a cabinet? How often will you be using your mixer? Kitchen mixers can be pricey, so if you are not doing a lot of baking because your primary product is no-bake coconut cookies, a good handheld mixer may be just what you need. On the other hand, if you are committed to baking cakes, pies, cookies, and homemade breads, you may want to select a heavy duty kitchen mixer. The cost will range from $15 to $60 for a handheld mixer to over $400 for a top-of-the-line professional model.

How to Select Cookware

Since you are about to become a serious home-based baker, you will need good quality cookware that gives you the best results and that will last a lifetime. Check your bank account. The best pots and pans are not cheap. Expect to pay between $150 and $500 or more for a set that has eight to ten pieces.

Here's what to look for:

- Start with a set that includes at least two 8-inch or 9-inch sauté pans, a 4- to 5-quart pot, and a 7-quart or larger stockpot; and augment your set with one or two 1-quart saucepans. Select cookware with thick-walled construction and riveted all-metal heatproof handles.
- Your cookware should come with some sort of lifetime warranty. Be wary of those that do not.
- A thermal spot in the skillet that turns red when the pan is hot is a good thing.
- Measuring marks on the saucepans are also helpful.
- A layer of copper in the base of a pan ensures perfect browning every time you cook.
- Consider contoured silicone handles with a thumb grip for comfort.
- Look for handles that stay cool.
- Get pots with spouts and lids that allow you to strain foods.
- All heavy anodized aluminum heats evenly and will last a lifetime.

If you are still not sure about what to purchase, ask someone whose cooking skills you admire and respect about the type of cookware they use and why.

Basic Cooking Equipment and Supplies

The list below is not all-inclusive, and there may be items that you do not have on hand and will not need depending on what you are baking. Don't fret; this is a basic listing of the different types of utensils and equipment used by home-based bakers. Cake decorating supplies are not included in this list since such supplies are dependent on the type of decorating a baker specializes in, along with the type of cakes that he or she prepares.

Aluminum foil

Blender

Bowls

Cake pans

Cake racks

Can opener

Carving board

Casseroles

Chopping board

Colander

Cookie sheets

Cutters (cookie cutters, biscuit cutters)

Dish cloths (dish towels)

Double boiler

Flan ring

Food mill (a tool used to grind and puree foods)

Food processor

Two- or three-prong fork (used for lifting food products out of a pan)

Funnel

Grater

Ice pick

Jelly roll pan

Cake knife

Chef's knife (a utility knife designed to perform many cutting tasks in the kitchen)

Paring knife

Serrated (bread) knife

Ladle

Lemon squeezer

Mandoline (a kitchen utensil used to cut foods at varying widths, even paper thin)

Measuring cups

Measuring spoons

Melon baller

Mixer

Molds

Mortar and pestle

Paper towels

Parchment paper

Pastry bags and tubes

Pastry board

Pastry brushes

Pepper mill

Pie server

Plastic wrap

Pot holders/gloves

Potato peeler

Poultry shears

Rolling pins

Rotary beater (for eggs)

Salt mill

Scale

Scissors

Scrapers

Silicone baking pads

Skewers

Spatulas

Spoons

Strainers

Thermometers

Tongs

Wax paper

Wire whisks

Basic Pantry Items

A home-based bakery kitchen is not complete until the pantry is thoroughly stocked with ingredients used for baking your specialty products. The following includes the essential herbs, spices, and staples that are needed to prepare a wide variety of home-based bakery products:

Dry Goods and Other Must-Haves:

- A variety of oils (olive, canola)
- Flour (all-purpose flour, wheat, rice)
- Evaporated milk (canned)
- Sweetened condensed milk
- Honey
- Sugar
- Sugar alternatives (Agave, Lakanto, Stevia)

Basic Refrigerator Pantry Items:

- Butter/margarine
- Cheese
- Milk or cream
- Eggs

Flavorings, Spices, and Spirits

Flavorings (lemon, maple, vanilla, and others) come in the form of extracts and artificial flavorings. Extracts are created by the process of distillation, extracting the essence of a compound; while an artificial flavoring is produced artificially. Flavorings are not natural products and are typically produced by fractional distillation and additional chemicals to manipulate the taste of a product.

Spices are strongly flavored aromatic parts of plants. When used in small quantities, they can pack a great degree of flavor to both sweet and savory baked goods. Spices are distinguished from other plant products used for similar purposes, such as herbs (green, leafy parts of plants), aromatic vegetables, and dried fruits.

Here are some of the more popular spices used by today's home-based bakers:

- *Cardamom*—Found in the form of a powder and seed. An Asian, Indian, and African spice used in many desserts and breads.
- *Cinnamon*—Found in the form of a powder and stick. There are two types of cinnamon: Ceylon cinnamon (also known as true cinnamon), which curls inward on itself from both edges when dried; and Cassia cinnamon, which has a more pungent smell. Cassia is also lighter in color and softer. Cassia is brittle and breaks easily and curls in on itself from one edge.

This is often sold in stores as Ceylon cinnamon, but don't be fooled, it is not true cinnamon.

- *Cloves*—Used to season soups, stews, and desserts.
- *Curry Powder*—Curry is best-known in Indian and Thai cuisine, but it is also found in other parts of Asia, in Africa, and in many other countries. Some of the spices in a curry may include but are not limited to the following: turmeric, coriander, cumin, cayenne or other chiles, cardamom, cinnamon, cloves, fennel, fenugreek, ginger, and garlic. Curries are used to flavor a variety of breads.
- *Ginger*—Used in some desserts, some meat dishes, and in Asian cuisine; found as root ginger, or in powdered and crystallized forms.
- *Nutmeg*—Used grated and ground in cakes, pies, cookies, breads, and pastries. It is always good to have a whole nutmeg and a grater on hand in your pantry.
- *Paprika*—A powder made from dried sweet red peppers, used in Hungarian cooking. Spanish paprika and Hungarian hot paprika are also available and used as a garnish on savory breads and buns.
- *Saffron*—The bright yellow, spicy powder or red threads come from the crocus flower. It is used to color and flavor a number of Mediterranean foods.
- *Vanilla Bean*—The husk of the bean is best stored in an airtight canister filled with sugar. This will make wonderful vanilla sugar for baked goods, such as cakes and cookies. To use, split and scrape out the little black seeds; this is where the true vanilla flavor originates. Used to flavor creams and desserts.

If you are interested in baking with wines or spirits, there are a few that you should have on hand. (Be sure to check with your local regulatory agency to verify that you can use alcoholic ingredients in your baked goods.)

- *Brandy*—Used in many chocolate cakes and bars.
- *Calvados*—Apple brandy, used with many fruit pies and tarts.
- *Framboise*—This expensive but worthwhile raspberry spirit does marvelous things to fruit pies and spice cakes.
- *Kirsch*—A clear brandy distilled from cherry juice and pits. It is most prominently known as a flavorful addition to cakes using dried fruits.
- *Madeira*—This wine is excellent in pound cakes.
- *Marsala*—A fortified Italian wine, Marsala is used as a dessert wine or after-dinner drink and is often used in pound cakes and spice cakes.

- *Rum*—Light rum is best for cooking and is great in desserts.
- *Sherry*—A sweet sherry brings out the flavor in butter cakes.

There are many other ingredients that can enhance your baked goods, and what you keep on hand will be dependent upon what you are selling. Just remember to purchase in bulk if you can afford to do so and rotate your products so you are using the oldest products first.

Many home-based bakers want to sell lots of different products. This is not always wise since the more products you plan to make, the more ingredients you will need, and that can get expensive. It is best to start with one or two products, build a following of committed customers, and add new offerings approximately twice a year as you build your business.

Organizing Your Pantry

As you begin to organize your pantry, you will start to wonder, "Is there enough pantry space for all my needs?" Fear not. This is the time to think about the product you want to produce and create a good plan for keeping your ingredients easily accessible.

It doesn't matter if you have a walk-in kitchen pantry, a smaller kitchen pantry, or designated kitchen cupboards. Regardless, it is smart to invest in a few simple pantry accessories to keep your items close at hand. For example, if you have deep cupboards, you might want to consider pull-out shelves, particularly if you have the types of shelves that force you to reach for an item every time you need it.

You may also want to consider placing items that are used often in a small basket—for example, measuring cups and spoons, spatulas and other small utensils, and frequently used spices. This allows you to locate these items quickly when setting up for food preparation.

When baking supplies are organized and placed where you can always locate them, your prep time can be dramatically reduced; and the sooner you can prep your ingredients, the quicker you can get your products into the oven.

Keeping your ingredients at eye level and within easy reach also eliminates the need to stretch and bend, which reduces potential mishaps. If you have shelves that are shoulder level, consider using a "lazy Susan," a sort of turntable that gently spins and provides easy access to items that are stored on it. Use it for small containers you use often, such as containers of flavorings or spices.

It is really not necessary for you to purchase fancy pantry hardware, such as magnetic spice racks or ceramic bowls. It is more important that your pantry is clean and functional, allowing you to locate the items you need quickly. The important thing to remember about pantry organization is that you need to have ample room for the products and the supplies you need to store. You might consider mounting tiny hooks and bars to the inside of your pantry door so you can reach certain supplies such as pot holders and kitchen towels with ease.

You may be storing canned and dry goods along with plastic bags, wax paper, and aluminum foil; just remember, your cleaning supplies must be stored separately and never with food products. You may even want to keep your cookbooks in an area away from food products so as to prevent them from becoming soiled.

Package and Label Requirements

All food products must be packaged in Food and Drug Administration (FDA)–approved food grade packaging. You must use food grade packaging for anything edible that you intend to package, store, and sell. A food grade container is one that will not transfer noxious or toxic substances into the food it is holding. If you are uncertain whether a package type is food grade, you can contact the manufacturer. Ask if the particular container is FDA-approved, meaning that it is safe for food use. When inquiring, be sure to specify the characteristics of the food you are storing: wet, dry, strongly acidic or alkaline, alcoholic, or with a high fat content. A container that is approved for one type of food may not be approved for another.

Your food grade packaging is designed to protect its contents from outside environmental influences, such as moisture, oxygen, heat or cold, light, insects, and/or rodents as well as preventing damage during handling and shipping.

Food grade packaging is everywhere. Every time you go into the grocery store, you are surrounded by it. Many well-known companies such as Tupperware and Rubbermaid manufacture and sell empty packaging for the express purpose of containing repackaged foods. The kinds of containers you are interested in and the types of foods you want to put in those containers will dictate where you need to look for a particular packaging system.

You may need to set up a simple quality assurance program to periodically analyze packaging materials and ensure that they are performing adequately. If you are shipping your baked goods, you will need to set up detailed procedures covering

Packaging Your Product

Home-based bakers must understand that food packaging is of enormous importance. How your product tastes is important, but consumers buy with their eyes and your packaging must be attractive, easy to open, and transportable. Packaging is a potential marketing tool, and it says a lot about your brand and who you are as a company. If you have questions about what type of packaging is best for your product, contact the regulatory agency that licensed your home-based bakery for more information.

When assessing how to package your product, you should:

- Present the baked goods in an attractive and desirable form.

- Use only FDA-approved packaging.

- Prevent light from striking the product if it could potentially damage the product (e.g., melting frosting).

- Use a label on which important information can be printed. Ensure that the label is large enough to include all required information and is firmly affixed to the product.

- Allow certain gases to escape from the package (e.g., in the case of bread).

- Make sure your packaging is resistant to breakage or other damage caused by rough handling.

- Use a product that is environmentally friendly whenever possible.

- Use tamper-proof packaging when necessary.

- Use the appropriate size and shape to suit the baked goods.

conditions under which your materials are packaged, shipped, and stored prior to use. Your regulatory agency can provide detailed information and guidelines.

If you are using plastic or clear, flat polypropylene food bags, you will want to make sure the bags are handled with clean hands or plastic gloves so there are no fingerprint smudges or debris on the bags. This may seem to be a small issue, but customers want products that look clean and unsullied.

State and/or local government agencies may have different packaging and labeling requirements. For example, the state may require that you package your products in a specific manner, while your local county may have a slightly different requirement. It is your responsibility to abide by both requirements. It may mean more work for you in the long run, but your goal is to satisfy the regulations of all relevant government agencies since those requirements are there to protect the consumer.

Planning Your Packaging

Home-based bakers often keep their packaging simple by electing to use FDA-approved pastry boxes. If you want to rise above the norm, simply check out the competition and answer the following:

- Describe the packaging used by your competition (jar, cardboard box, plastic, colored, plain white, etc.)

- Describe your anticipated product package type. Is it similar to your competition, or are you thinking outside the box using something unique, yet FDA-approved?

- Is the proposed package easily available or something that will need to be special ordered? (This is important, particularly if you have a large order to fill and run out of your special-order boxes.)

- Is special handling needed for your product? How will that affect your packaging? Will your packaging protect your baked goods from breakage if dropped during shipping?

- Does your package design conform to federal and/or local regulations?

There are products that do not ship well and will easily break. For example, large, thin cookies are more likely to break in transit than small, thick cookies. If a cookie is moist, it may dry out before it reaches its destination. Some bakers use royal icing (often made with egg white), which dries hard; however, most regulatory agencies will not allow the use of raw egg white, so you will need to contact your state/local regulatory agency to see if it is an approved product. There are home-based bakers who place a commercial brand of frosting in the shipment so customers can frost their own cookies. I would not recommend this, but it has been done. Last, you may want to avoid using anything chocolate since chocolate melts and is not reliable. And cookies that are filled must be wrapped carefully so they do not arrive broken.

Home-based bakers specializing in baking cookies will want to remember that, depending on the type of cookie you are shipping or selling, you may want to package the cookies three to a bag, allowing space for them to breathe, but not packed so loosely that they get jostled around and break. Packaging is a delicate balance and works best if you go through a number of test shipments to friends and family in distant places. If you do not receive the results you want, shipping your product may not be possible or you may need to change your product to one that is better suited for being shipped.

The best cookies for mailing are drop cookies, refrigerator or icebox cookies, molded cookies, and some no-bake cookies. Brownies and unfrosted bars also ship well. If you are concerned about the flavors blending with others in the shipping box, pack cookies in separate containers or wrap the different types separately within a container. Again it is necessary that you send out trial shipments to ensure the products arrive the way you want.

Cookies and Bundt cakes may be shipped in sturdy, foil-lined containers, or tins. It may be necessary to place waxed or parchment paper between cookie bars, cushioning them but also keeping them snug. You may place shredded paper, packing peanuts, or other packing materials below, above, and between containers to cushion them within the shipping box. This material should never touch the actual food product, however, since it may not be FDA-approved.

Seal the box with shipping tape and cover the address label with clear tape for protection, unless you are using a special label for shipping. Mark the package clearly with the word PERISHABLE to encourage careful handling. Remember during cold and hot weather you will want to make sure your product arrives in the best possible condition, so talk to your carrier about the best way to ship during adverse weather conditions. Some home-based bakers do not ship specific products during extreme weather conditions because they cannot guarantee the product will arrive in an acceptable condition.

You will want to contact a local carrier, such as FedEx, UPS, or the USPS, and provide them with information about your specific product. Let them know what you are shipping and that you want the items to arrive undamaged. Often these carriers will provide suggestions on the best ways to package your products.

Food labeling is required for most prepared foods, including breads, cereals, canned and frozen foods, snacks, desserts, and drinks. The product label is placed across the front of the product and the ingredient label across the back of the product unless otherwise directed by your state/local regulatory agency. Do not place labels under a product so that the customer must turn the product upside-down in order to read it. You may also use one large label to display both the product and ingredient information, if it's allowed by your regulatory agency.

Nutritional Labeling

Most home-based bakers do not need to put nutritional information on their products; however, if you want to put this information on your product, there are a number of government and private organizations that will work with you to provide that information either for free or for a small fee. The regulatory agency that licensed your home-based bakery can supply more information about nutritional labeling.

The FDA Small Business Nutrition Labeling Exemption for nutrition labeling exemptions can be found at www.fda.gov/Food/GuidanceComplianceRegulatory Information/GuidanceDocuments/FoodLabelingNutrition/ucm053857.htm and applies to retailers with annual gross sales of not more than $500,000 or with annual gross sales of foods or dietary supplements to consumers of not more than $50,000. For these exemptions, a notice does not need to be filed with the FDA.

Basic information that should be placed on all home-based baked goods may include but is not limited to the following:

- Name of the product
- Name and address of the manufacturer
- Phone number/Web site/e-mail address
- A list of all ingredients in descending order by weight

- Net weight of the product (customary and metric)
- Allergens that may exist in the product, such as nuts, dairy, etc.

An accurate scale will be needed to weigh your products. Make sure you can place the entire product on the scale for weighing. If the scale is too small, the product will not fit and you will not get an accurate weight. Direct any specific questions about product weight to your regulatory agency, since there may be specific guidelines you will need to follow.

There are times when you will use a product with multiple ingredients. You will need to list all the ingredients in the product; for example vanilla extract might look like this on a label: Vanilla (water, alcohol 38 percent, and vanilla bean). Some regulatory agencies may direct you to list the product differently, so always refer to your regulatory agency. It is not necessary to identify your bakery as a "home-based bakery" unless directed by your regulatory agency. There are some agencies that insist you state "not prepared in a state-approved commercial food facility." If you are required to place that on your product, you must do so.

Sample Label

Peanut Butter Chocolate Chip Walnut Cookie
The Cookie Dough Laydee, 5555 Caryville Street, Cary, NC 27519
1-866-555-5555
www.thecookielaydee.com
   Ingredients: enriched bleached flour, brown sugar, white sugar, peanut butter (roasted peanuts and sugar, 2 percent or less of molasses, partially hydrogenated vegetable oil (soybean), fully hydrogenated vegetable oils (rapeseed and soybean), mono- and diglycerides, and salt), semi-sweet chocolate chips (sugar, chocolate liquor, cocoa butter, soy lecithin, artificial flavor, and milk), butter (cream, salt, and milk), eggs, walnut pieces, soda (sodium bicarbonate), salt (calcium silicate, dextrose, and potassium iodide), vanilla flavor (water, alcohol (38%), and vanilla beans). Net wt. 16 oz.
   May contain nuts and/or nut meats.

The regulatory agency that licensed your home-based bakery will provide specific guidelines for the language you should use concerning food allergens. If you would like to read more about what the FDA requires in this regard, visit the Guidance, Compliance and Regulator Information Web page atwww.fda.gov/Food/LabelingNutrition/FoodAllergensLabeling/GuidanceComplianceRegulatoryInformation/default.htm.

Transporting Your Products

Product transportation may be vital to your home-based bakery business. When you are producing small amounts of baked goods, it may not appear difficult to deliver them, but it depends on what the products are and how carefully they have been packaged. You want to make sure the products are placed on a level foundation

Transporting a Tiered Cake

If you are transporting a tiered cake, you will want to take note of the following:

- Do not assemble a tiered cake until you reach the wedding hall or venue.

- Transport each tier on its own, either in a cake pan or placed directly on a nonslip mat.

- Find out the distance between the venue and your starting location.

- Allocate ample time (at least 3 to 4 hours) before the event begins, to allow for getting to the venue and assembling the cake.

- Drive your vehicle slowly and avoid sudden jerks so you do not damage the cakes.

- One way to avoid damage from sudden jerks is to place the cakes on non-slip mats.

- Remember to bring all your cake decorating tools with you in a tool caddy.

- Bring extra cake and icing and extra flowers to replace any broken or damaged ones.

- Always bring a camera with you and take a photo of the assembled cake before you leave.

and do not rock from side to side. You will want to nestle your boxes between one another or place them in a large box that does not allow for much movement. There is nothing worse than arriving at a delivery location only to learn that your baked goods are damaged.

You are not above the law, so make arrangements to park in an approved drop-off area. If you have to call ahead and have your customer meet you, make arrangements. It defeats the purpose if you sell a product, and then get a ticket for parking in a no-park zone. Keep your driver's license and insurance with you at all times. You would not believe the number of stories from bakers who stepped out of their cars for a moment to drop off products, only to return to find a parking ticket on the windshield.

Customer and Vendor Relationships

Good and bad service begins with you. As a home-based baker, you will deal with customers on a weekly or sometimes daily basis; and whether you are selling your products wholesale or retail, it is your responsibility to provide a clean, unobtrusive location for selling your products.

When selling from local farmer's markets or other state-sponsored locations, you may be asked to follow certain rules and regulations. Many farmer's markets or farm stands may limit the types of products you can sell, or they may ask for proof that your kitchen has been inspected and/or licensed and proof of ample product liability insurance. There really is no way to get around this, and you shouldn't, since these requirements protect both you and your customers.

Honesty is the best policy. If your home-based bakery business is restricted to selling online cakes, cookies, and bread, do not go against the regulations and sell cheesecakes or other products that you are not supposed to be selling.

Dishonesty can destroy any business relationship instantaneously and irrevocably. Circumventing proper channels to make a sale can put a serious strain on a customer-vendor relationship. If a customer asks about a product you cannot legally produce, tell them the truth. If you open your brick-and-mortar location or start baking from a kitchen incubator that allows you to prepare cheesecakes, then you can contact that customer and let them know what new products are now available.

As with any business, there are unprofessional, unethical vendors, preparing products that are not allowed and selling them "under-the-table," so to speak. There will always be those who do not abide by the laws of the land. This book will hopefully help keep you honest and aboveboard; abide by the rules and regulations set by your state/local regulatory agency and operate a government-approved home-based bakery.

Maintaining open, sincere communications with your customers is vital to developing strong vendor-customer bonds. When a business owner works hard to determine and meet the needs of his or her customers, it shows in repeat business. Building a strong customer base is more difficult for home-based bakers than traditional bakeries. Most of your potential customers don't know you even exist, so word of mouth and exhibiting professional and ethical business practices will go a long way in building a loyal and steady clientele.

It is easy to undercut other bakery businesses in your community, but remember, cost competitiveness ensures only a short-term sales victory; building trust, providing a quality product, answering the telephone when it rings, and returning e-mails promptly show that you value your customers and the importance of building lasting relationships with them. Strive at all times to do the right thing.

Getting Started

Starting a home-based bakery is not unlike any other home-based business. The major difference is that your kitchen is your work area, and it may be necessary to create an office space where you can pay bills, address telephone or e-mail inquiries, and attend to any other business matters associated with your home-bakery business. Let's take a detailed look at what is involved in starting your home-based bakery from a structural viewpoint.

Every home-based bakery will be different, since each baker is baking a different product that will focus on the needs and wants of their particular customers. A cake decorator who only prepares celebration cakes will structure her business differently from a pie baker who focuses on preparing pies for various civic league fundraisers. It is essential that you tailor the information in this chapter to suit the specific needs of your bakery.

How to Structure Your Home Bakery Business

A home-based bakery is structured in the same way as any other small home-based business and takes on some of the same responsibilities as a brick-and-mortar facility. You will have legal concerns, liability insurance, maintenance of equipment and appliances pertinent to your baking business, and any cost associated with employees—should you decide to have paid helpers during peak production times.

One of the first decisions you will make in starting a home-based bakery is how to structure your bakery business. Depending on the circumstances surrounding your specific business venture, you have six options. The differences between these options are based on the degree of individual liability and how each one is subject to taxes. The six basic business structures are:

- **Sole Proprietorship**—The baker owns the company and is responsible for both its assets and liabilities.
- **General Partnership**—The baker contracts with one or more people to run the business with equal responsibilities and liabilities.
- **Limited Partnership**—Some of the partners in the bakery partnership have less interest and liability in the company. In this type of partnership, there must be at least one general partner.
- **Limited Liability Company**—The baker structures the company so that the baker and the people with whom the baker is starting the business have less or limited liability.
- **C Corporation**—The baker who sets up a traditional corporation has little or no personal liability.
- **S Corporation**—The baker has the same liability aspect as a C corporation. The difference is the way it is taxed. C corporations are taxed twice, once on the corporate level and again on the personal level. S corporations are only taxed on the personal level.

You may be hesitant to invest in financial and legal assistance in making this decision because accountants and attorneys are expensive. However, you need to make the right decision the first time, so you should seek professional advice when deciding how to structure your business. Your local Small Business Administration

Small Business Administration

You may contact your city/state/county legal aid society or Small Business Administration Office to obtain assistance in setting up your business structure. (www.sba.gov/localresources/district/nc/index.html)

Additional assistance may be obtained from:
    Local legal clinics
    State Bar Associations
    State or local business service organizations
    LawHelp (www.lawhelp.org/)

can assist you, or you may want to also speak to a SCORE counselor—a personal business coach responsible for helping you with every step of your business development. You can locate a SCORE office in your area by visiting www.score.org/findscore/index.html.

Other Legal Considerations

You may also want to secure an attorney to address any other legal matters that may arise from running a bakery out of your home. Due to zoning restrictions, many communities will not allow customers to purchase products directly from your home, so you will need to contact your local zoning department to see if there are any restrictions. For example, I lived in Cary, North Carolina, and I was restricted from having customers come to my home to pick up their baked goods. I decided to tack on a small delivery fee and deliver baked goods within a designated delivery area.

There are many home-based bakers who set up their business at local farmer's markets, farm stands, and flea markets or who sell directly to food co-operatives; never take a chance with having a customer come to your home to pick up a product if zoning does not permit it. If the individual has a mishap on your property, you are liable. Always follow the rules set by your zoning department. The safety of your customers and your company should always be a priority.

Insurance

Before starting operations, you will need to look into various insurance options, such as general liability, public and/or personal injury, and products and completed operations insurance, which covers a contractor's liability for injuries or property damage suffered by third parties as the result of the contractor completing an operation. For example, if you are operating from a licensed commercial kitchen facility (kitchen incubator or shared-use kitchen) and you start a fire, you would need completed operations insurance in order to be properly covered.

Public and/or personal liability insurance is essential if you are selling your product at a farmer's market or other facility outside your home. If a potential customer leans on the table where you are showcasing your lovely pound cakes and he falls, you could be sued. This is not anything you want to skimp on, so the more coverage the better; this is not the time to purchase the bare minimum in liability coverage.

It is unlikely that you will address workers' compensation insurance; however, I mention it because during certain holidays some home-based bakers bring in temporary workers. It doesn't matter if they are full- or part-time; if you have people working for you, workers' compensation insurance coverage is essential. In some states you cannot operate a business without it, so make sure you contact your state department of labor. You can also locate worker compensation resources by state at www.workerscompensationinsurance.com/links/index.htm.

Recalls

Numerous recalls on food products over the past few years have prompted the federal and state governments to reexamine food recall procedures and institute workshops and educational programs that will assist food workers in developing a way to trace and recall food products that might carry foodborne illness. As a home-based baker, it is your responsibility to also have a food recall plan in place if the peanut butter or honey you use in your baked goods is recalled.

In fact it is not just about tracing the products and recalling them; the food recall plan also needs to be implemented on a regular basis to ensure it is a viable and effective system in facilitating trace-backs and recalls before a problem erupts.

The purpose of recall procedures is to withdraw products that are already in the marketplace. A home-based baker should be able to track all products used in the production of his or her baked goods. There should be records, such as supplier identification and production and distribution records for a specific lot of product, e.g., cases of peanut butter, nuts, dried fruits, etc. These records should be organized, properly maintained, and easily retrievable in less than one hour.

Every state food recall plan is different, but there are standard procedures that will help in tracking recalled foods. This is not an inclusive listing and it is imperative that you follow state or local health department and/or department of agriculture requirements for recalling defective products.

- Identify the product involved
- Provide the reason for the removal/correction of the product and date the deficiency was discovered
- Provide the total amount of products produced with the deficiency
- Estimate the total amount of product distributed to the public
- Provide distribution information (who received the products)
- Propose a strategy for conducting the recall

Should a product you use be recalled, hold the recalled product using the following steps:

- Segregate the product, including any open containers, leftover product, and food items in current production, including items containing the recalled product.
- Mark recalled product "Do Not Use" and "Do Not Discard." Inform all staff or bakers working with you not to use the product.
- Obtain accurate inventory counts of the recalled products from every feeding site, including the amount in inventory and amount used.
- Account for all recalled product by verifying inventory counts against records of food received at the feeding site.

It is also important that you test your ability to retrieve this information from your records by conducting mock recalls. There is no doubt this will involve more labor and time, but it is essential that you be able to locate the lot coding on packages by date code or other coding to initiate the recovery of a particular product in the event of a recall.

Food Recall Resources

Food Recall Changes

www.foodpoisonjournal.com/2009/06/articles/food-policy-regulation/changes-on-the-horizon-for-food-recall-procedures/

Army Food Recall Manual

http://fycs.ifas.ufl.edu/foodsafety/2005/adobe/Food%20Recall%20Manual-KS.pdf

USDA Food Recall Fact Sheet

www.fsis.usda.gov/Fact_Sheets/FSIS_Food_Recalls/index.asp

Sample Standard Operating Procedure for Handling a Food Recall

http://sop.nfsmi.org/HACCPBasedSOPs/HandlingaFoodRecall.pdf

A lack of records or the inability to recall product records will not only call your production procedures into question, but it could put consumers at risk for illness. Again, you will want to contact your individual state health department, department of agriculture, or food regulatory agency for current state recall guidelines.

How to Organize Your Office

One of the most important features of good office organization involves its functionality. All too often our offices are crammed with office machines, equipment, supplies, or worse yet, whatever random items don't have a place anywhere else in our homes. As a home-based baker, you will need an office space where you can address the daily needs of your business.

If you do not already have a computer, you may need one, particularly if you are going to design your own labels, business cards, and marketing materials. It's no secret that operating a home-based business allows you to keep your overhead low, but unlike most home-based businesses, as a baker you will have the added expense of putting more wear and tear on your oven, microwave, and refrigerator, increased utility bills, and sometimes placing a strain on the needs of your family.

To make the most of my office space, I've organized my recipes so they are always just a short reach away, and I've maintained folders on my computer desktop of all important documents and forms needed to operate my home bakery.

Your office supplies and expenses may include some of the following items:

- Computer
- Printer
- Telephone, dedicated telephone line, and answering machine or voicemail
- Internet connection
- Bookshelves
- Cabinets with drawers for storage
- Pens, pencils, paper clips
- File folders
- Labeling supplies
- Package and shipping supplies
- Calendar and/or daily planner
- Basic accounting software (e.g., cake matrix pricing tool for costing out your cakes)
- Calculator

There may be additional office supply items that you will need, and you will have time to obtain these items as your business grows. There is nothing wrong with making do with what you have until you start making enough money to purchase additional business supply needs.

I once met a home food processor who made bamboo pickles and explained that, when she did not have enough money for professional labels, she photographed her product and used a photo printer to make photocopies of the product. She used the Photoshop program to add her contact information and passed the photos out to inquiring customers. The postcard-size photo was perfect when setting up samples at farmer's markets and gourmet food shows. So when it comes time to create marketing tools for your home-based bakery, remember that unique and creative trumps expensive every time.

Kitchen Office Essentials

Home-based bakers have two responsibilities in their kitchen. One is to bake the product, and the other is to test new recipes. You will need to organize your kitchen (or "laboratory" as I sometimes like to call it) in such a way that you can not only prepare your product but also experiment with new and exciting recipes.

If you have room in your kitchen for the items you will need to create new recipes, by all means do so. As you experiment with different recipes, you will need to keep a notebook on hand along with a list of resource Web sites, cookbooks, reference books, and a camera, as some bakers like to record or videotape the creation of their new recipe.

Remember that your kitchen must also be used by your family members; therefore, it is important to make sure your business supplies and all materials associated with your bakery have a place to rest undisturbed when not in use. There is nothing worse than learning that your ten-year-old used your new recipe as scratch paper for his math homework, so organize and store important documents accordingly.

Your kitchen should be clean and free of clutter. Thoroughly scrub down and organize your cabinets. Repaint them, if necessary, to give them a fresh look. Remember, you are cooking for the public, and you want to assure the compliance agent inspecting your kitchen that you are providing a clean environment in which to bake your products. All cabinets in your kitchen are subject to inspection.

Provide separate storage for dry goods and equipment used for your business. Supplies used to produce your home-baked goods and the equipment used to

Home-Based Bakery Compliance Checklist

The following sample compliance checklist may be used by a home-based baker who is required to submit to a home kitchen inspection by the state or local compliance agency. The list is not all-inclusive and may not list all the compliance requirements, so contact your agency for a complete listing.

Sample Compliance Requirements	Check here if compliant
Kitchen: Clean, free of clutter, and organized. You may want to clean and organize your cabinets thoroughly and in some cases repaint, to give them a clean fresh look. *Remember you are cooking for the public and you want to assure the compliance agent that you are supplying a clean environment in which to bake your products. All cabinets in your kitchen are subject to inspection.*	
Kitchen: Provide separate storage for dry goods and equipment. A separate area should be provided for storage of products used to produce your home-baked goods and the equipment used to prepare those goods. Separate from the food and cooking equipment used by or consumed by your family.	
Kitchen: A separate area should be provided in the refrigerator for refrigerated items, e.g. butter, eggs, etc. It may be a separate shelf or one of the bins in your refrigerator. Separate from the food consumed by your family.	
Kitchen: All ingredients should be stored in air-tight containers or plastic jars or glass jars. Storing your ingredients in air-tight containers assures they will be kept bug free. You may use zip lock bags but they should be heavy duty to avoid punctures and rips.	
Write or type your recipes and include a list of the ingredients for each recipe; this will assist you when it is time to design your labels. The compliance agent may want to see your recipes and/or a list of the ingredients; along with a sample product label.	

prepare those goods must be kept separate from the food and cooking equipment used by or consumed by your family.

Refrigerated items used for your business—e.g., butter, eggs—should be kept separate from the food consumed by your family. You can designate a separate shelf or one of the bins in your refrigerator for these items.

All ingredients should be stored in air-tight containers or plastic or glass jars. Storing your ingredients in air-tight containers ensures that they will be kept bug-free. You may use ziplock bags, but they should be heavy duty to avoid punctures and rips.

Write or type your recipes and include a list of the ingredients for each recipe; this will assist you when it is time to design your labels. The compliance agent may want to see your recipes and/or a list of the ingredients along with a sample label.

If you are working with an incubator or shared kitchen facility, an office space may be provided there. You should be aware, however, that not all rented kitchen facilities allow you to keep your work materials at the facility, since maintaining those items in a secure location may not be possible.

Writing a Business Plan

Anyone interested in securing investors for their business will need to create a *formal* business plan, for which professional guidance from financial and legal experts is a must. As a home-based baker, you will need a *modified* business plan that can act as a road map to guide you in developing your bakery business.

Your modified business plan will be written using the same format as a traditional business plan, and may have the following components.

- **Executive Summary:** You may want to write your executive summary last, since it will highlight the overall key focus areas of your bakery business.
- **Company Description:** Legal establishment, history, start-up plans, etc.
- **Product or Service:** Describe what you're selling. Focus on customer benefits.
- **Market Analysis:** You need to know your market, customer demographics, customer needs, and how to reach them, etc.
- **Strategy and Implementation:** Explain how you will manage your business and what responsibilities you will have. Make sure you can track results. You need to know that what you are doing works!
- **Web Plan Summary:** For e-commerce, include discussion of Web site, development costs, operations, sales, and marketing strategies.

- ■ **Management Team:** Describe your organization and the key management members; if you are working alone, document everything you will
  be responsible for. If you have helpers, even volunteers, document their
  responsibilities.
- ■ **Financial Analysis:** At the very least, make sure to include your projected
  profit-and-loss and cash flow tables. This may be difficult for some home-
  based bakers in the beginning. You may need to operate your home-based
  bakery for six months to a year before seeing consistent cash flow.

Sample Home-Based Bakery Business Plan

The Small Business Administration provides sample business plans and instructions
on how to write a business plan. Visit: www.sba.gov/smallbusinessplanner/plan/
writeabusinessplan/index.html.

    This is a sample business plan that has been modified for home-based bakers. It
is not often that home-based bakers need to secure funds to start their home bakery
business; however, you will want to create a plan describing how you will operate
your bakery and what will need to be done to get it up and running. The effort put
into the planning process will pay off in the long run. If you want to create a vision
of where you are going the information below will prove helpful.

Step 1

Determine what type of product your community not only wants but needs. Pay
attention to what is missing in the marketplace. Have you heard of anyone complaining about a lack of this or that? Is there a new product idea that could fill this
need?

Step 2

Do a bit of product research to find out if your new product idea has been tried
already. Check around at local bakeries, farmer's markets, and other locations where
homemade baked goods are sold.

Step 3

When you have a solid new product idea, locate or create a recipe that produces a
superior product.

Step 4

Now it's time to create a sample product and offer samples to the public. You may also want to design packaging and a label and take a photograph of your product.

Step 5

Test your new product and have the public, family, and friends share their opinion of the product in its entirety—e.g. flavor, texture, color, taste, package appeal, etc.

Step 6

After you've properly designed your new product, it's time start the marketing process and decide how you will take yours product from kitchen to market.

Choose a Legal Structure for Your Business

You may or may not need legal assistance to create the legal structure of your business; however you must decide if yours will be one of the following:

- Sole Proprietorships —Doing Business As (DBA)
- Partnership—Doing Business As (DBA)
- LLC (Limited Liability Corporation)
- INC (Incorporated)

You may contact your city/state/county legal aid society to obtain assistance in setting up your business structure or contact your local Small Business Administration office.

Additional assistance may be obtained from:

- Local legal clinics
- State Bar Associations
- State or local business service organizations
- LawHelp (www.lawhelp.org)

Tax Concerns

Contact your state and local tax authorities to learn about small business tax responsibilities.

The IRS (Federal Taxes) provides a detailed Web site to address your small business tax questions: www.irs.gov/businesses/small/article/0,,id=99336,00.html. The phone number for Telephone Assistance for Businesses is 1-800-829-4933. Hours of operation are Monday–Friday, 7 a.m.–10 p.m. your local time.

Business Insurance

Liability insurance for your business and product is essential. You need to be honest with your insurance agent and disclose exactly what type of food products you will produce.

- General Liability Insurance
- Personal Injury Insurance
- Worker's Compensation and Disability
- Products Insurance and any other coverage that addresses the production of your products and services, including any coverage needed to operate in a kitchen incubator facility or sell at a farmer's market

Annual Premiums for food-product liability insurance coverage may be $300 and up, and the following may impact your insurance premium:

- Level of gross sales
- Level of coverage
- Type of market (specialty, retail, wholesale)
- Type of product
- Recall plan (if applicable)

Executive Summary

Write this last. It is a paragraph or two of highlights about your business.

> *The Happy Cupcake Bakery (HCB) is a start-up home-based bakery retail establishment located in Virginia. The bakery expects to attract customers from affluent counties outside Baltimore, Maryland, and the District of Columbia. Most of the customers will special order signature cupcakes for special events, weddings, and charity gatherings. HCB will also offer celebration cakes for anniversaries, birthdays, and weddings. HCB's main*

competition will be three local commercial bakeries in Baltimore; however HCB offers gluten-free products, something no other bakery offers at this time. After establishing the home-based bakery, HCB will look for a traditional brick-and-mortar location sometime in 2012. The company was founded by Brenda Happy and her husband, a baker in the United States Navy. The two bakers will operate the bakery from their home kitchen (part-time) on weekends and may bring on casual labor assistants during peak baking times (e.g., during the holidays), for weddings, and when catering dessert buffets.

HCB will not need a loan for start-up and opening day is planned for December 1, 2010. While the small home-based bakery has the potential to grow rapidly, the first two years will be spent establishing financial stability and increasing market share.

Company Description

This includes legal establishment, history, start-up plans, etc. You may include as much information about your company and the staff as necessary. In some cases a home-based bakery will have one staff member, the baker, and that is sufficient; just remember to provide information about your background, even if you are self-taught.

The Happy Cupcake Bakery is a sole proprietorship and is established to provide quality cupcakes, celebration cakes, and a number of gluten-free cakes for customers in the community. The two bakers at HCB have approximately twenty-four years of experience between them and both have worked in commercial bakery establishments. Mr. Jim Happy is a full-time baker who works the night shift for a grocery chain in the Maryland area.

Product

Describe what you're selling. Focus on customer benefits.

The Happy Cupcake Bakery will provide a variety of cupcakes, eighteen flavors, not including gluten-free cupcakes and celebration cakes. HCB will be known for its quality and unique flavors.

Market Analysis

You need to know your market, customer needs, where they are, how to reach them, etc. Some bakers may not perform a formal market analysis. Although it is helpful in learning what the needs are in your community, you may start a home-based bakery without one.

> *There are currently no bakeries in the community by HBC that offer gluten-free cupcakes. Based on a free survey posted last year on the HBC Web site using SurveyMonkey (www.surveymonkey.com), the owners of HBC discovered that there was a need for gluten-free cakes in the community, specifically cupcakes.*

Management Team

Describe your organization and the key management members; if you are working alone, document everything you will be responsible for. If you have helpers, even volunteers, document what they will be responsible for.

> *The primary management members at HCB are the two bakery owners. They will be responsible for business developments, baking, marketing the business, sales, addressing all customer service needs, and the overall operations of the home bakery business. The specific duties have not been assigned, however, the owners will set those responsibilities by September 1, 2010. The owners of HCB do not foresee additional staff coming onboard at this time.*

Financial Analysis

Home-based bakers may want to create a Profit and Loss and Cash Flow tables. You may visit http://profitandlosstemplates.com and download free profit and loss templates when you are more familiar with what you will be selling and how much you will gross. The Web site also offers a tutorial for new business owners who want to learn more about understanding the financial health of their company.

As a home-based baker, you may want to use this modified business plan as a resume and present it when renting incubator space or when applying to become a vendor at the local farmer's market. In most cases, this business plan is created to keep you on task as you build your home-based bakery business and perhaps later if you decide to take your business to the next level.

By writing your business plan, you illustrate a clear vision for your business and demonstrate on paper that you have a solid concept on which to operate a financially successful home-based bakery. The business plan forces you to focus on what you are trying to achieve, precisely where you want to be over a specified period of time, and exactly how you plan to get there. If written properly, a business plan will encourage you to take a serious look at the expenses you will incur, your projected sales, monthly expenses of operation, and the volume of business you generate from month to month. This information will allow you to make decisions about whether your business is growing and moving in the direction you want to go.

For example, if you are interested in only operating your bakery part-time and you want to gross a minimum of $1,000 per month, you will need to know how many cakes must be sold to meet that monthly goal. If your pound cakes sell for $30 per cake, you will need to sell roughly thirty-three cakes a month or about eight cakes a week to come close to your goal. This is an average, and as a home-based baker, you will soon learn that there will be weeks when you are busy and others when you are not; but you should always strive to meet your monthly goal. The moral of the story: Plan your work and work your plan.

04 Starting a Legitimate Home-Based Baking Business

The idea of baking from home and selling to the public is nothing new. Can you remember going to local farmer's markets and flea markets as a child and asking your mom for money to buy homemade cookies? Today the practice of home-based baking has been brought under more scrutiny due to the many foodborne illness issues making the news, but like commercial establishments, home-based bakery businesses are required to follow strict food processing rules and regulations. The unfortunate truth is that many bakers do not bother to learn about the regulations associated with operating a home bakery. They either don't know the regulations exist or they are afraid that by contacting compliance authorities they will bring attention to an operation that is not following the rules. My motto is "Better safe than sorry"; it is better to know how to operate a legitimate home-based bakery than operate it on the wrong side of the law. Don't you want to sleep better at night knowing you are operating within the legal guidelines?

In this chapter we'll discuss some of the parameters involved in baking from home for profit. The fact is you are feeding the public and you'll have to follow food-processing regulations, zoning laws, and state and local government policies regarding what you bake and how it is prepared. There will be liability issues to consider, and it is your responsibility to follow all government-mandated regulations to protect both you and your customers.

Why You Must Follow the Law

There is a certain degree of due diligence on the part of every home-based baker prior to starting a home bakery business. When I first started to learn about the laws regulating home food processing I discovered that not all government agencies communicate with one another, in fact they rarely do. The local health department did not know the rules for starting a home-based bakery and immediately informed me that baking from a home kitchen was illegal. I then decided to go to my local farmer's market where I saw other bakers selling their products on the weekend. I spoke to the market manager and learned that the regulatory agency for home-based bakeries was not under the jurisdiction of the health department but the state Department of Agriculture. He explained the state "cottage law" allowed me to sell my baked goods at any state-sponsored farmer's markets. I was overjoyed and on my way to starting my own home-based bakery business.

What is a Cottage Food Production Operation?

A cottage food production operation involves a person using their home kitchen to produce food items that are not potentially hazardous, including but not limited to bakery products, jams, jellies, candy, dry mixes, spices, and some sauces. Cottage laws are different for every state, and there are states that have no cottage laws at all, instead mandating that bakers use only licensed commercial kitchens for food production.

A cottage food production operation may or may not be exempt from inspection and licensing. For example, in the state of North Carolina, a compliance officer from the North Carolina Department of Agriculture and Consumer Services will come to the baker's home and inspect it. That is not always the case in other states; however, many food products, including those produced and packaged by a cottage food production operation, may be subject to home inspection, food sampling, and testing to determine if the product is misbranded or contaminated. I know you may be thinking this is a lot of regulation for something as simple as sugar cookies, but it is the law, and every state has a different law regarding the operation of a home-based bakery.

I shared this home-based baking information with friends outside the state of North Carolina only to learn that, indeed, every state is different and most government employees within their own departments did not know what the law said about home baking or if their state even has a cottage law. Imagine my shock when I moved to Georgia and was told by a state department of agriculture official that I might want to take copies of the "cottage law exemption" with me to the state-sponsored farmer's market. He was not sure if the information about home baking had filtered down to most of the farmer's markets across the state.

Let's face it, as a home-based baker, it is your responsibility to investigate the home food processing laws in your state, city, and county prior to starting your bakery. It is easy to get excited about someone wanting to pay you cold, hard cash for your luscious chocolate chip cookies or butter pecan pound cake, but the truth is there's a bit of homework you must do before putting up the OPEN FOR BUSINESS sign.

Restrictions: A Part of the Business

There are a number of restrictions that may creep up when first starting your home bakery business. Reading the guidelines set down by my regulatory agency, I learned that I could not make the signature cheesecake that my family and friends loved so much. The cheesecake was considered a potentially hazardous food product since it needed to be refrigerated after baking, and my home refrigerator did not comply with the state requirement.

You may also need to evaluate your water source, which must be a "safe source," meaning the water used must be transported and dispensed in a sanitary manner. If your water source is municipal, nothing further may be required; however if your water source is private (i.e., it is from ground water or surface water), then it must be inspected and tested annually. This will be different for each community, so check with the regulatory agency in your area.

Home-based bakers can only prepare what their regulatory agency deems to be safe (i.e., not potentially hazardous) food products, such as baked goods, jams and jellies, certain candies (not chocolate), dried mixes, and spices. Potentially hazardous foods, such as chicken pot pies or pesto, must be produced in a licensed commercial kitchen or facility separate from your home. I'm sure someone somewhere is saying, "I know a lady who makes cheesecakes, and she's not baking in a licensed commercial kitchen." All I can say is, I'm glad I'm not her, because she is operating outside the law and putting herself and her customers at risk.

Some regulatory agencies also require that each and every recipe for each individual product be reviewed by a food processing authority, so check with your regulatory agency before selling any baked goods to the public. This review is done to make sure the product does not have any potentially hazardous ingredients and is both labeled and packaged properly.

The idea of selling cookies to the public appears easy and does not seem as though it should involve a lot of oversight, but every aspect of your product must be documented. This means you must have a standard recipe with exact quantities (in grams of weight, not volume) and exact temperatures and times for processing that you use on a regular basis. Some agencies may even ask you to bring them a sample of your product, the recipe with exact ingredients, and your preparation procedures, noting baking times and temperatures.

When the compliance officer came to my humble home bakery, she inspected every area that involved the production of my pies: the kitchen, the dining room where I did my packaging, my office, and the bathroom closest to the kitchen. I lived in North Carolina at the time, and the compliance inspector was in my home for over an hour, asking questions and making sure I understood the rules and regulations for operating my home-based bakery. What did she want to see? A list of ingredients used for each product to be sold, sample packaging, and a sample label completed in the format recommended by the North Carolina Department of Agriculture and Consumer Services. (The rules and regulations for operating a home-based bakery in North Carolina, for example, can be viewed at www.agr.state.nc.us/fooddrug/food/homebiz.htm.) Home-based bakers must contact their state health department or state department of agriculture to learn if home food processing is allowed in their community.

You might ask yourself, "Why all the guidelines?" Remember, you're feeding the public. Your regulatory agency wants to know that you are developing a product that is fit for human consumption and that you're not attempting to deceive the public or feed them substandard food. If you say you are selling a jumbo chocolate chip cookie made with specific ingredients and weighing eleven ounces, they may want to see it and weigh it. Some other government restrictions might include:

- Only selling products from a state-sponsored farmer's market (prepared in accordance with market rules and restrictions)
- Only selling products grown on your farm (if you own a farm)
- Only selling products approved by the state/local regulatory agency
- Only selling products that are "not potentially hazardous" (i.e., baked goods, certain cakes, pies, cookies, and breads)
- Only selling products prepared in a licensed commercial kitchen facility

Never let restrictions like these deter you from your dream. If your product is delicious, people will find you. There are numerous home-based bakers who just bake on the weekends and sell at the local farmer's markets for extra income and some who use the farmer's market as a pickup point for customers using online orders and prepaying. There are a number of creative ways to market your baked goods, and this will be discussed in more detail in Chapter 6.

As I interviewed home-based bakers across the country, I found that many are family-run bakeries specializing in one or two products. Today more bakers are becoming interested in preparing organic products and products that are wheat-, gluten-, dairy-, and sugar-free. What I learned most from my own compliance inspection is that it really does not matter how many products you sell as long as you are following the rules and regulations set by your regulatory agency.

Zoning Issues and Home-Based Baking

Abiding by local government zoning laws is also important, so be sure to check out your local zoning laws and contact your compliance agency for details. In my hometown I was told that, although I could bake from home, I could not have my customers come to my home to pick up their baked goods.

The issue was that the zoning department didn't want customers parking their vehicles in front of the homes of my neighbors or blocking driveways; they did not want the added activity to be seen as an annoyance—similar to a home mechanic who has customers bringing their cars to his home for repair all day and night. There are some streets that are zoned for both residential and commercial use. Contact your local zoning office to make sure you can operate your home-based bakery and see if there are any limitations to having customers pick up their products from your home.

When I was not able to meet with customers at the local farmer's market for pickup, I decided to simply increase my price a bit to incorporate door-to-door delivery costs, and most of my customers were none the wiser. In this way I did not have to explain the reason for a delivery charge. Of course, depending on where you live, you may have to ask for a separate delivery fee, so do what works best for you. Another strategy you might want to consider is setting up a pickup point at your local farmer's market or food co-op if it's allowed by your regulatory agency and zoning laws. Some of the home-based bakers I interviewed for this book recommended asking independent coffee shop owners if their shop could be used as a pick-up point. One baker had so much business at the coffee shop, the owner asked to sell her products at the shop since her customers were bringing in her products and ordering coffee.

Liability Insurance: Mandatory Coverage

There really is no way to get around liability insurance if you want to sell your baked goods at the local farmer's market or food co-op; insurance is an indispensable expense. This includes general liability, product and personal injury liability, coverage on any rented space used for your baking business, equipment, vehicle, and worker's compensation for any employees you may hire. Insurance is there to protect you from unexpected mishaps. Many wholesale and retail vendors will not allow you to sell your homemade goods in their establishments without full liability insurance coverage; and some customers won't buy from you unless you are fully insured. Today the public is becoming more knowledgeable about home-based baking and other food businesses (especially with the rapid growth of farmer's markets) and rightly so.

In legal terms, the word *liability* refers to fault. The person who is at fault is liable to another because of his or her actions or failure to act. It is important to consult an attorney and an insurance agent to learn more about liability insurance as it relates to your home-based bakery. The rates for insurance depend on the state in which you live, the type of coverage you request, the agency you select, and the type of products you bake. So, be sure to shop around.

It is unlikely (not impossible) that you will be able to sell your products to retail or wholesale vendors without liability insurance; but why would you ever want to bake without insurance? I found through my own experience that one of the best ways to determine how much insurance you need is to ask the regulatory agency that inspected your kitchen or contact the manager of the farmer's market where you plan to sell your goods. Both should be able to tell you the minimum amount of insurance coverage needed. Securing insurance through your homeowner's policy may be quite expensive, and it may be best to seek an outside agency for a separate policy covering your business. I was fortunate to locate an affordable policy by talking to my banker. The policy was in line with the coverage needed to sell at the local farmer's market, and it covered my home-based bakery business and my products.

Developing Policies and Procedures

Developing policies and procedures that describe how your home bakery will operate is imperative to its success. I learned this the hard way. If you are not an organized baker and business owner, you will find operating a new business frustrating. Fortunately this is no different from operating any home-based business where you are responsible for providing your customers with quality products or services.

Operating a home-based bakery can be complex if you do not plan your work, work your plan, and set boundaries concerning when you will bake, what you will bake, and how often you take your products to market.

It is important to devise policies and procedures surrounding your everyday activities. You may think this is not necessary, particularly if you are baking a single product, such as red velvet cake. I learned that, by establishing sound policies and procedures, I was able to structure my baking days and operate in a consistent manner by preparing the right number and amount of products, thereby reducing waste and saving time. Following sound procedures also taught me to be consistent, and consistency is the key to operating a successful food production business.

Your customers will want your lemon pound cake to taste the same way every time they order it, and that cannot occur if you are not following strict guidelines in its preparation, packaging, labeling, and even delivery. Nobody wants to receive a cake that was baked on Monday and delivered on Thursday, particularly if your turnaround policy is twenty-four to forty-eight hours. The following are the business policies and procedures I put into place when operating my business. Every baker is different, so as you read through the policies, think about your own specific needs.

Commitment to Privacy Policy

A commitment to privacy policy explains to customers how you will use their contact and payment information both online and offline. I did not pass this out to my customers; however, I did have it handy on my computer in the event that a customer asked about what I do with their credit card and contact information.

Refund Policy

A refund policy explains how you will compensate your customer if there is an issue with the product or service they received from you. It is up to the individual home-based bakery as to whether they will offer a refund for baked goods. Many home-based bakers offer to replace the product as opposed to offering cash. This may pose a problem if customers pay with credit cards and customers may wish to withhold payment because they are not satisfied.

Freshness and Storage Policy

A freshness and storage policy provides customers with information explaining the shelf life of the product purchased. If a pound cake has a date stamp that explains

"Best used before January 5, 20XX" it is the customer's responsibility to use the product prior to the expiration date. Other cautionary statements you might use include: "Discard after [specified date]" or "Do not use past XX/XX/20XX." This policy is no different from that used by commercial food vendors who place expiration dates on perishable products such as bread, milk, cheese, and yogurt.

Company Guarantee

A company guarantee simply states that you stand behind your products. Do not create one unless you are willing to guarantee your product. For example, if you guarantee that you will always deliver your cakes warm from the oven by a certain time, do so; not holding to a guarantee is hazardous to the financial health of your business.

Online and Offline Order Policy

There are a number of home-based bakers who take orders via their Web site or e-mail. If you are going to take online orders, create a policy that dictates when you will acknowledge the online order and deliver the product. I learned the hard way that computers have a tendency to lock, lose information, and potentially create havoc for your business. If it *can* go wrong, it *will* go wrong, so you want to create an online order policy that allows you enough time to address any issues that may arise and still process the order with ease so customers receive their product in a timely manner. It is recommended that you seek legal advice when drafting your online and offline order policy so there is no misunderstanding with customers about how you will handle their orders.

Terms Policy

Terms are specific conditions that apply to all customer orders. For example, one term might address that, in the event of a product shortage requiring a product/ingredient exchange, you will not be responsible; another might state: "A $10 delivery fee will be charged for cakes delivered outside the metropolitan area."

Prices and Products Policy

A price and product policy addresses your right to change prices without notice and to introduce new product varieties and substitute products in the event you run out of stock.

Recall Policy

There have been numerous recalls on food products that have not only made Americans ill but in some cases have been lethal. The issue has prompted the federal and state governments to reexamine food recall procedures and institute workshops and educational programs that will assist food processors in developing a way to trace and recall food products that might carry foodborne germs and other impurities.

In fact, it is not just about tracing the products and recalling them. Your food recall plan also needs to be implemented on a regular basis to assure it is a viable and effective system in facilitating trace-backs and recalls before a problem erupts. In the state of North Carolina, for example, the North Carolina Department of Agriculture and Consumer Services sponsored a workshop to assist small food processors in developing a recall policy and procedure. If you would like to learn more about how to establish a food recall policy and procedure contact your state department of agriculture. Below is a simple recall policy that assures customers you are willing to be responsible for addressing the food safety needs of your customers and will abide by all state regulations regarding food recall procedures. This can be posted on your Web site.

Sample Recall Policy

As a commitment to our customers, The Yummy Cupcake Bakery acknowledges it is our responsibility to effectively organize and manage the recall of any food used in our products that has been demonstrated to be unsafe or unsuitable. The recall coordinator for the bakery has been given authority from management to make recall decisions on behalf of the Yummy Cupcake Bakery.

We will recall and advise the community about all recalled products incorporated in our baked goods, working in accordance with state/local recall laws and regulations, implementing a recall action plan that will keep our customers safe from harmful products. When a recall is initiated, our actions in recalling the affected food/s need to be coordinated with the state department of
_____. [Insert the regulator agency for food recall in your state/county.]

Customer Contact Procedures

Customer contact procedures are imperative. Are you taking orders over the telephone? Are you taking e-mail orders, or do you have a Web site storefront? No matter what process you use, everyone in your family who answers the telephone or may come in contact with a potential customer via e-mail or the Internet (or even at the front door) will need to know how to address customers when they call.

You may want to create a phone script or a responder e-mail message each time someone inquires about ordering your products. Have you decided how soon you will return phone calls and e-mails and what is your turnaround time from the placement of an order until delivery? There is no hard and fast rule; however, I recommend that you respond to all phone and e-mail inquiries within 24 hours of receipt, if at all possible. It's good standard business practice.

Product Development Procedures

Most home-based bakers start their business by producing a favorite family recipe. I had approximately five types of pies I baked around the holidays: pecan, sweet potato, chocolate, lemon, and pineapple. I started out with the pecan pie and later learned that my original recipe would only take me so far, and I found myself itching to add new products. For example, let's say you make dark chocolate brownies, do you think dark chocolate brownie lovers might enjoy the addition of pecans or walnuts?

Remember, your kitchen is your laboratory. It is the place where you put on your apron and take on that Julia Child stance, ready to jump right in and create something magical. All too often bakers get caught up in the day-to-day baking responsibilities; but where you are now will not take you to where you need to go in the future. So, the innovative process must be ongoing, and there should be some rhyme and reason behind how you develop new products. You don't have to innovate daily, weekly, or even monthly, but be sure to set aside some time during your home-based baking journey to commit to experimenting with and creating new products. Creative ideas are all around you; take time to look and see what trends are on the horizon. Is it red velvet donuts, pumpkin scones, or a new chocolate chip caramel cookie? Remember, a lack of creativity in product development is one of the best ways to bring your business to a grinding halt.

A Sample Recipe Style Sheet is a wonderful tool that can be used to document every aspect of your recipe. It allows bakers to jot down little tidbits of information

Sample Recipe Style Sheet

Develop a style sheet for all recipes. A style sheet can be as simple as a piece of notebook paper with notes scribbled on it, or as organized as a photocopied form with spaces labeled alphabetically for easy reference.

RECIPE	YIELD (Number Of Servings)	BAKING TEMPERATURE (Recipe Features)
Peanut Butter Cookies	1½ dozen cookies (18)	Bake at 350 degrees for 8 to 10 minutes
Ingredients		
½ cup shortening (Crisco)	½ cup butter	1 cup sugar (white)
1 cup dark brown sugar, firmly packed	1 cup creamy peanut butter	2 eggs (large)
2½ cups all-purpose flour	1 teaspoon baking powder	1¼ teaspoons baking soda
½ teaspoon salt	1 teaspoon vanilla extract	
Preparation Directions		
1. In large bowl, cream shortening, butter, and sugars until light and fluffy. (The mixture may have a hint of graininess when rubbed between fingers)		
2. Add peanut butter and eggs and cream well.		
3. Sift together dry ingredients		
4. Add dry ingredients to peanut butter and egg mixture.		
5. Stir in vanilla extract. Dough should be stiff.		
6. Drop 1 tablespoon of cookie dough on baking sheet; leave 1½ inches between cookies.		
7. Bake at 350 degrees for 8 to10 minutes. (Centers should be soft for a chewier cookie.)		

Sample Recipe Style Sheet (blank)

RECIPE	YIELD (Number Of Servings)	BAKING TEMPERATURE (Recipe Features)
Ingredients		
Preparation Directions		
Special Instructions		

that can go wrong with a recipe and provide an opportunity to write suggestions that will make the recipe better and sometimes tastier. I usually type my style sheets after my stint in the kitchen (lab) experimenting; and save the style sheets in a folder on my computer desktop. I also print a copy of the sheet and place it in a plastic protector sleeve to prevent soiling while I work in the kitchen.

Kitchen Maintenance Procedures

Maintaining your kitchen in peak working condition is sometimes easier said than done, since your kitchen also doubles as the primary location for family food preparation. The regulatory agency that inspects your kitchen for home baking may ask that you not use the same utensils and supplies used to prepare family meals. If that is the case, you will need to create a way to keep business supplies separate from everyday use. I assigned separate cupboards for my business supplies and separate shelves in my refrigerator and food pantry for all the ingredients used for my baking business. If you are not sure how to organize your kitchen, speak with your regulatory agency representative. Often they can tell you what has worked for other home-based bakers in your community.

It may also be helpful to write out instructions on how to use specific kitchen appliances, especially if you have a family member or friend who comes in from time to time to assist you in preparing your baked goods. Don't ever assume everyone knows how to operate your appliances. This will avoid mishaps and accidents in the kitchen. It goes without saying that a first aid kit is invaluable in your home kitchen, since accidents can occur whether you are baking for your family or for profit.

Food Safety and Sanitation

Understanding how to keep your kitchen free of contamination is critical. Food safety is an increasingly important public health issue. Every state government has rules and regulations surrounding food handling and home food processing. It is your responsibility as a home-based baker to keep your food production area clean and sanitized.

Some of the rules may appear to be common sense, but remember there are times when sense is not common to all; these rules, regulations, and limitations are put into place to prevent foodborne illness. Foodborne illnesses are defined as diseases, usually either infectious or toxic in nature, caused by agents that enter the body through the ingestion of food. If you are not familiar with the food safety regulations in your state, you may want to enroll in a food sanitation course. Check with your local health department or state department of agriculture for course availability.

There are also online courses available at www.servsafe.com, one of the nation's leading authorities on food safety education. Additional resources for food safety information are available from FoodSafety.gov, an information-filled Web site provided by government agencies that offers an "Ask the Expert" phone line and live chat. Visit www.foodsafety.gov/ for more information.

Less Toxic Homemade Household Cleaners

All-Purpose Household Cleaner
Add 1 teaspoon liquid soap to 1 quart warm water. This solution can be used for a multitude of cleaning jobs including countertops and walls.

Oven Cleaner
Add 2 tablespoons of baking soda to 1 gallon of water. Scrub with very fine steel wool (found in home improvement stores). Wear gloves and rinse well, then towel dry.

Mildew Cleaner
For mild cases combine ½ cup white vinegar and ½ cup water in a spray bottle. The acid in white vinegar is a powerful mildew remover.

Vinyl Floor Cleaner
Add ½ cup vinegar to 1 gallon water.

Glass Cleaner
Add to a spray bottle: 1/2 teaspoon liquid soap, 3 tablespoons vinegar, and 2 cups water. For very dirty windows, add more soap.

Label cleaning mixtures clearly. Never put them into old food containers or store them near foods. If you do use chlorine cleaners or bleach, do not mix them with ammonia, acids, or any other cleaning products or it will produce a deadly gas!

Indoor Pest Control

Pesticides are designed for one purpose: to kill bugs. Both the active agents of most pesticide products and the solvents in which they are dissolved pose health hazards to you, your family, and your pets. The use of pesticides indoors is particularly risky. People often use pesticide products without regard for the proper safety precautions. Ventilation in many homes is relatively poor and people spend many hours a day at home.

Prevention

Cockroaches, ants, weevils, mice, flies, and other common household pests all have three things in common: They need food, water, and a place to call home. To keep them out of your home:

- Eliminate food sources by storing food in the refrigerator or in tight-fitting containers. Don't leave dirty dishes out overnight. If pet food is left out, place the dish in a pan of soapy water.
- Use garbage cans with tight-fitting lids.
- Freeze cereals and flours to eliminate food pests.
- Eliminate water sources by fixing all leaking sinks, faucets, and pipes.
- Eliminate hiding places.
- Caulk cracks and plug holes where cockroaches hide. A good silicone caulk is the longest lasting. Duct tape can be used for a quick fix.
- Clean out all food and paper storage areas regularly.
- Don't let pests into your home in the first place. Keep screens on doors and windows in good repair.
- Control ants outside by spraying their nests with insecticidal soap.
- Prune back branches that provide a bridge into the house.

Monitor your pest populations to learn the normal levels present and to discover when they are becoming a problem. When preventative methods are not providing enough control, use the least toxic control methods.

05 Pricing Your Products

One of the biggest thorns in the side of a home-based baker is the issue of pricing products. The simple truth is no one can tell you with any certainty what to charge for your baked goods. Setting the price structure for your cake, pie, cookies, or pastries is one of the most difficult parts of any baking business.

You can almost compare baked goods to real estate: The price of a cake, pie, or batch of cookies varies widely by location and usually reflects what the local market will bear. Narrowing down the right price for your product requires research of your competitors' prices and a firm understanding of your own costs. This is difficult if you are purchasing ingredients at retail prices, so make every possible attempt to purchase your ingredients wholesale or from bulk food companies. Seek to secure the lowest prices possible for your raw materials.

When you first start out in the home-based baking business, it is easy to think you should not be asking the same price as experienced bakers in the community. Don't sell yourself short. Your customers are looking for quality products at a fair price, and they often will do business with whoever can deliver the best goods at the lowest prices.

How to Price Your Products

In the field of home-based baking, you must have a tough skin and be confident in your abilities. It is only natural to think that you are not as good as bakers who have been around for ten or twenty years, but don't get stuck there or you will never move forward. The first person that must value what you have to offer is you. If you exude confidence, it will show up in your food, your face, and your attitude.

A consultant who works with food entrepreneurs recently shared with me that she tells her clients to use the pricing method that involves charging two or three times the cost of the ingredients. If this happens to be the method you are currently using, you may wish to reconsider. The method is not derived from any sound accounting practices and may cause you to underprice your baked goods.

When pricing your product, you must include the cost of:

- Every ingredient
- Your labor
- Your overhead (packaging, labels, and any other items that make the product attractive)
- Your utility cost
- Your personal needs (health insurance, liability insurance, and other "silent" costs)

In other words, you must include everything!

Some bakers don't think itemizing the cost of every little ingredient is helpful. There are home-based bakers who only consider the big-ticket items like expensive chocolates or Danish butter; this unfortunately will never give you an accurate cost for the product. The base cost of your baked good may be $6, however for those who include every aspect of the cost going into the production of the product, the cost could easily rise to $8 or $9; it is important to consider all cost associated with the production of your baked goods.

So what is really most important when pricing a product? In Adam Smith's 1914 classic *The Labor Theory of Value,* he states: "The real price of everything, what every thing really costs to the man who wants to acquire it, is the toil and trouble of acquiring it. What everything is really worth to the man who has acquired it, and who wants to dispose of it or exchange it for something else, is the toil and trouble which it can save to himself, and which it can impose upon other people."

What does all that mean? The value of a product increases in proportion to the duration and intensity of labor performed in its production. So, though you may work diligently to produce a beautiful wedding cake or ten exquisite loaves of bread, you will gain greater value from producing greater quantities of your quality products.

The moral of the story: The more product you can deliver, the more valuable the product becomes. In other words, preparing two wedding cakes for $500 each is good, but preparing ten wedding cakes for $500 each is better. It is important that home-based bakers understand that the amount of product they can prepare in a home kitchen will be limited and, if they are to increase the quantity of product they produce, they will have to either bake for longer hours or move to a larger baking facility, both of which will affect the bottom line. This is one reason why I continue to remind home-based bakers that this may be a part-time venture because increased revenue comes from increased volume.

One advantage of operating a home-based bakery is that it provides time for bakers to build their business and customer base, and perfect their products. Bakers interested in transitioning to a brick-and-mortar establishment now have experience selling product to the public, operating a small business, maintaining inventory, and possibly working with outside vendors. These are all attributes loan officers will want to know about when seeking capital for a brick-and-mortar business venture. It is possible for a home-based baker to outgrow the home kitchen and seek a larger facility to meet the business's growing needs.

One major error made by home-based bakers is comparing their cakes to cakes from a retail store or gourmet bakery. There is no comparison; it's like comparing apples and oranges.

Home-based bakers are a unique group. The products you prepare should not be like anything in a grocery store or neighborhood bakery. Your products are not made in bulk, they are custom-made to order and therefore are special to the customer who orders them. Think of it like ordering a custom pair of boots—the customer's foot must be measured so the fit is perfect; a home-based baker prepares custom-baked goods that are not available everywhere (or at least we hope they're not); and special products demand a special price, so again don't sell yourself short.

As you develop your home-based bakery business, ask yourself how much do you make per hour at your current job? How much money do you need to make per hour to live the lifestyle you are currently living? These are important questions, and many home-based bakers make the mistake of not thinking through their home-based baking plan. At some point you must be realistic and ask yourself how feasible is it to think you can make your baking business a full-time occupation or even a part-time job.

Once you have figured out what hourly rate will work best for you, the next step is to figure out approximately how much time it takes for you to make your baked goods. You need to have a clear idea of how much time most products take to prepare and bake. If you are a cake decorator, the time adjustment may be more critical, depending on if you are decorating a 9-inch, three-layer birthday cake or a five-tier wedding cake. Knowing what your time is worth will help you determine the final price of your baked goods.

According to Indeed.com, depending on where you live in the United States cake decorators earn about $500 per week depending on their skill, number of hours worked, and experience in the industry. The rule of thumb is usually the more involved the cake, the longer it will take you to decorate. How you calculate your wage is based on the individual. There are some bakers who do not calculate an hourly rate because you will never be paid the amount of time and effort put into the product; and all products are priced differently.

One example I can share shows how a home-based baker figured how many products she would need to bake to bring home her current gross income. At the time she was working a part-time job, grossing $400.00 per week. Let's do the math assuming she sold cupcakes by the dozen for $25.00 per dozen.

$400.00 / $25/dozen = 16 dozen cupcakes

She would need to sell 16 dozen cupcakes per week to gross what she was making from her part-time job. Sixteen dozen cupcakes is 192 cupcakes. Does this sound realistic? It is if she is selling retail to an office complex cafeteria that has asked her to deliver roughly 5-6 dozen cupcakes three times a week.

There is a lot of thought that must go into addressing how much your home-based bakery will gross and the calculations are tricky. Some bakers use a cake matrix pricing tool that allows you to calculate your cost, time, supplies, and ingredients. You may need to talk to a number of home-based bakers to come up with a method that works for you.

Wholesale vs. Retail Production

The question to sell wholesale vs. retail is not a difficult one. If you want to make quantity sales, then you should consider selling your products wholesale. Unfortunately this is difficult to do if you are baking from home, since most home kitchens only have one oven.

If you are preparing your products from a commercial kitchen incubator with multiple ovens, you may have an opportunity to prepare more products and sell to several commercial vendors. Many home-based bakers feel they are being taken

My Wage

I bargained with Life for a penny,
And Life would pay no more,
However I begged at evening
When I counted my scanty store;
For Life is a just employer,
He gives you what you ask,
But once you have set the wages,
Why, you must bear the task.
I worked for a menial's hire,
Only to learn, dismayed,
That any wage I had asked of Life,
Life would have paid.

—Jessie B. Rittenhouse,
My Wage, The Door of Dreams

advantage of by wholesalers, since most wholesale vendors want to get their baked goods at the lowest possible price.

The rule of thumb is to start selling retail, directly to the customer, and consider wholesale distribution only after you are sure you have the kitchen capacity to produce products in bulk. This is why it is so important to price your products appropriately and market to the proper demographic.

What Is a Profitable Product?

You make the product profitable. You must have personality, passion, and perseverance—the drive that makes you move forward even when you feel like you want to stop and call it quits. Oh, it also helps to have a deliciously dynamic product!

You need to ask yourself:

- Do I believe in my product(s)?
- Do I believe in my ability?
- Do I like making this product?

If there were only one thing in life you could do to make a living . . . is this it? Stepping into the shoes of a business owner is tough, real tough, and you need to know you are ready. What happens if your product takes off in a direction you are not prepared for and hundreds of orders come in?

A profitable product has:

■ Strong market demand
■ Simple, easily accessible ingredients
■ Reasonable production time
■ Affordable packaging
■ Exceptional presentation
■ Customers willing, ready, and able to buy the product
■ A product that complements other goods on the market

What you want to bake may not be what your customers want to purchase, so there may need to be a bit of a compromise. In a perfect world our customers would enjoy and purchase every product we make, but we don't live in a perfect world, and you will need to be realistic about how to satisfy your customers' wants and needs in relation to the goals of your business.

A profitable bakery product is one that the community wants to buy on a consistent basis. This is one reason why the cake decorating business has become so popular. Not everyone has the funds to purchase a cake from the high-end Charm City Cakes in Baltimore, Maryland, but everyone wants a beautifully decorated cake for their special event. I have yet to hear a bride-to-be say, "Oh, just give me the plain butter cake with plain white frosting."

Any product can be a profitable product if you take time to do market research and pay close attention to what is missing in the market. Are you going to focus on a particular niche (e.g., kosher, gluten-free, sugar-free baked goods, or vegan baked goods)? How many products will you offer? You are a small home-based bakery, and the more products you bake, the more ingredients you must invest in and have on hand.

After deciding on the types of products you will offer, you need to decide on the preparation specifics of each item. If you are making cakes and cookies, will you sell certain cookies during the spring and summer months and others during the fall and winter? Or will you sell every product year-round?

Select the recipes you want to use and take an inventory of the foods you will need to purchase. You may find that some products are currently too expensive or will need to be sold online because the customer demographic at the local farmer's market may not pay $18 for nine perfectly packaged chocolate truffle brownies. You will need to review all of these areas if you are going to control cost and make a profit.

Knowing the Rules of Competitive Pricing

The rules of competitive pricing can be a challenge during tough economic times. Let's look at this scenario. While setting up your stand at the local farmer's market, customers are quick to inform you that they have obtained a better price for an organic carrot cake with butter cream maple frosting from a vendor three tables down. What do you say? Is this true or just a bargaining tactic?

You need to understand the pricing structure of your competitors and determine if they are just undercutting you by a dollar or are they really pricing their product significantly lower? It might be beneficial to determine the actual demand for your product, if possible. Often, if there are a number of home-based bakers selling the same product in the same location, someone is sure to offer their baked goods at a considerably lower price while offering their best seller at a higher price or introducing a new product at 20 percent higher than it should cost.

This is when you need to contact your network of home-based bakers and see what's happening. (You do have a network of home-based bakers that offer thoughts and opinions, right?) Don't work in a vacuum. There is enough business out there for everyone, but you have to know the rules to the pricing game lest you get left behind.

It's no secret that doing the research to price properly is time- and labor-intensive. However, during any economic cycle, the work you put into getting it right will significantly affect your revenue and profits (and satisfaction) in the long run. My recommendation is to join a number of baking message boards and post a message preferably to bakers in your own state and community. This gives you an opportunity to see how other bakers are devising a price for their products. You may also want to view information on the Cake Boss cake pricing software to assist in pricing your products.

Locating your competitors involves finding everyone who also bakes from home in your community. You may want to visit Find-A-Baker.com to view a listing of bakers in your area. Assessing their Web sites or giving them a call to see if they are home-based may be helpful. Visit various farmer's markets, farm stands, and flea markets to see what is being sold and start paying close attention to flyers posted in community centers, public libraries, and church bulletin boards. Home-based bakers are everywhere and once you are on the lookout you will starting seeing their marketing materials more and more.

Baking Message Boards

Real Baking with Rose: www.realbakingwithrose.com

Cake Central: http://cakecentral.com

The Fresh Loaf: www.thefreshloaf.com/

Wilton Discussion Forums: www.wilton.com/forums/

06 Marketing Your Home Bakery Business

Attracting new clients can be a challenge, since many patrons are a bit skeptical about eating foods prepared from a private home kitchen. As a home-based baker, it is your responsibility to educate your customers and let them know you are a licensed, insured, legitimate business.

It is not necessary to embark on an expensive campaign to market your home bakery, and you don't have to spend a lot of money on ads, brochures, and Web sites. The best source of new customers is your current roster of satisfied patrons. When customers are pleased with the products you offer and the service you provide, and they walk away feeling they received a great product at a fair price, they are bound to return and to tell their friends.

In fact the best way to get these word-of-mouth referrals from your current customers is to:

- bake great products
- if you deliver, deliver on time and within budget
- provide a high-quality product
- be reliable and dependable
- thank or reward your customers whenever they give you a referral for new customers, e.g., 10 percent off their next order

There are really no magic marketing plans or answers to how you bait customers and keep them returning again and again. There are many variables that go into effectively marketing your home-based bakery, and we will discuss some of them in this chapter. These marketing strategies are not all-inclusive, and as you operate your home-based bakery, you will learn that some marketing ideas work better than others. So, always be prepared to think outside the box, try new approaches, and abandon any strategies that are not working for you.

Defining Your Home Baking Niche

In today's competitive business climate, you've got to separate yourself from the crowd. You've got to create a niche. By offering something no one else has and by targeting your business to a few select markets, you protect yourself not just from the competition, but from the twists, turns, and plunges of the economy.

By creating a product that completely fills a need, your customers will have a hard time imagining life before you came on the scene. Is there a niche that your competition has failed to fill? Can you perhaps become a specialist in an area where there are many generalists? The most successful marketers are those with specific expertise in a particular area.

Finding your own niche is often a matter of putting a new spin on what you already do. Ask yourself, how can I differentiate my home-based bakery from others? How can I create the perception that my market simply cannot live without me? What do I have to offer? *Hint:* Think seasonal. Think healthy. Think comforting. Think outside the box.

Decide who you want your customers to be. Carefully choose your focus. If you have trouble, then examine the needs of your customers. Do you live in a college town? What are they searching for? Match what you're selling to what the customers want to buy. Make sure your niche is special, unlike anything else out there. Make sure your niche is viable. Is there a market? Is it a strong one? Anyone can bake cupcakes, but what about offering the "bakers dozen" of thirteen different types of chocolate cupcakes or custom cupcakes?

Tracking Trends

So, what are some of the more popular home-based baking products sold today? A review of food trend articles and home-based baking Web sites clearly shows that the types of products are as varied as the bakers themselves. However, the most popular products sold by home-based bakers today are pound cakes, custom decorated cookies, brownies and bar cookies, and a variety of candies, such as toffee, truffles, and fudge.

Developing a small home-based bakery involves paying close attention to food trends and what is not on the shelves (and ought to be) at gourmet food stores. This can work both ways—the baked good may not appear because no one wants it or because no one is making it, and it is your responsibility to do a bit of market research and learn which is correct.

Your first thought may be, "I just want to bake from home and sell to my community, I don't want to get into all that research stuff." Well, you need to know what people in your community are buying, and you won't know unless you do a bit of research. It's not as difficult as it may appear.

You can obtain information about product research by:

- Speaking to the managers of local farmer's markets and learning what has sold well in the past
- Contacting the perishable food manager at gourmet shops to learn what they are having difficulty locating for sale in their bakery or dessert shop.
- Using Google Alerts to learn about new upcoming food trends in the field of baking.
- Using Google Trends to learn about specific food trends that are popping up all over the globe.
- Subscribing to the *Gourmet Retailer,* an online magazine that tracks food trends. Visit www.gourmetretailer.com/gourmetretailer/index.jsp to subscribe to their free newsletter.

The demographic shifts currently underway will create both challenges and opportunities for home-based bakers. One of the biggest changes taking place is the aging of the baby boom generation. With just over seventy-eight million people born between 1946 and 1964, baby boomers are quickly redefining every stage of life, and they are of a generation that appreciates homemade baked goods and cakes, pies, cookies, and pastries made from scratch.

Home-based bakers would do well to consider catering to older consumers and providing baked goods that are gluten-free, products for diabetics, and cakes made with sugar alternatives. Remember, because someone is growing older does not mean they want food without flavor and texture. Home bakers may also want to pay close attention to the wants and needs of multicultural families. According to the Nielsen Company, more than 50 percent of families with children will be multicultural by 2025, and that number will rise to 60 percent by 2050. What does this mean to the home-based baker? It means that this is a wonderful time to visit ethnic bakeries in and around your community and take a peek at what is being offered. You may very well get in on the ground floor of the next fad in baked goods!

Positioning Your Products

To position your product successfully, you need to know the key benefits of your product. You then need to know:

- What your target market wants
- What benefits you can offer that your competition cannot

Then use this information to position your product. Publicize these benefits in all of your marketing materials.

There are several ways to effectively position your product:

- By price
- By attribute
- By application
- By solution

Price is the easiest way for consumers to compare you to your competition—people know the difference in cheesecake price when they're choosing between The Cheesecake Factory and Susie's Cheesecake Bakery.

Positioning by *attribute* is common in the automobile industry. For example, Mercedes emphasizes quality and elegance, while Jeep emphasizes its off-road rugged ability. You may highlight homemade goodness with no additives or preservatives, while a Wal-Mart cake may not be able to make that claim.

Positioning by *application* focuses on what the product will be used for. Folgers coffee, for instance, is positioned as being the best choice for morning coffee. You may make the claim that your organic granola bars are the perfect afternoon pick-me-up, loaded with organic dried fruits and nuts, perfect for adults and children alike.

Lastly, a *solution* positioning strategy can work extremely well. Since public education does not have the funds for extra tutoring to help children stay up to speed with their math skills, Sylvan Learning Centers have solved this problem by offering after-school tutoring programs. If you are interested in using online wheat-free products, dairy/nut-free products etc., your Web site might be the educational hub for those interested in learning more about such products.

The positioning options are endless, and you can choose to emphasize whatever aspect of your product you want. Whatever you want consumers to think of when they think of your bakery is the message you need to develop and communicate as effectively as possible.

Market Research

Let's review this scenario: You are currently working for someone else, and you have an idea for a new pound cake. The question you are asking yourself is, "Should I quit my job and start a new business to sell this product?" The sub-question is "Will this idea work?" If the idea is going to work, and you can make a significant profit by starting the business and selling the product, then starting the new business is something you should consider. If not, then starting a new business is probably the wrong decision. To start your new business, you will need to quit your job, perhaps get a second mortgage on the house, work incredibly hard getting everything going, and so on. If the idea does not work after doing all of that, it will be a major disappointment and potentially a big financial loss. Before you ever jump ship, do your homework and do it well.

Somehow you need to reach out to potential customers and/or current customers and find out what they are thinking. You need to ask questions and get some concrete answers. Do people need the chocolate toffee or celebration cakes you are offering? If so, how many people need it? Which features are important to these people and which are not? What price would customers be willing to pay, and why?

The process that you use to get answers to questions like these is called *market research*. There are two ways to look at the process: From a business standpoint, market research is a way to get answers to important questions before investing a lot of time and money creating a new product or service. From a consumer standpoint, there are many people who enjoy being a part of the market research process and they will sample your product for free all day and all night, telling you what you want and need to hear.

Let's go back to the earlier employment situation we examined. You are currently working as an employee, and you have an idea for a new pound cake. Let's say it's a new dessert of the month club, or an organic granola bar that you can pack in a lunch box, perhaps it's even custom decorated cookies. How do you find out if anyone wants or needs your product?

Short of manufacturing the new product and selling it to see how many people buy it, there really are only two ways to answer marketing questions ahead of time. You can find out directly or indirectly.

Let's look at the direct way first. To find out if people like your idea, you have to talk to them and see what they are thinking and feeling. You've probably been talking to people all of your life, so you are familiar with the many different ways to reach them. You can:

- Call people on the phone
- Talk to people face-to-face (Set up a table at the local farmer's market or flea market)
- Send an e-mail
- Send a letter through the mail
- Assemble people in a group, bring samples, and talk to them about your product

No matter which technique you are using for market research, your goal is to ask a set of questions and get feedback. What this will provide you with is:

A) A set of answers to your questions, and/or

B) New ideas. This is important because you will learn things that you never thought about by talking with people. For example, you might find that no one in the South wants your boysenberry pies, but in Southern California, they are a huge hit! This can be a big revelation— it can save you a ton of money that would have been wasted advertising your product in Florida or Texas, when it should have been marketed in California.

The indirect way to learn about the marketplace is to look at what's already out there. How many home-based bakers are making a competing product? What are their products like? How do they market them? What do they taste like? The fact that there is a competing product tells you that there are some customers out there, and you can access your competitor's market research by looking at the products your competitor is producing—assuming, that is, that the competitor did any market research.

Ask these three questions:

1. Who, if anyone, has a real need for the product you propose to sell, and how many of those potential customers are there?
2. How much, if anything, are they spending to address that need today (and/or how much would they be willing to spend)?
3. Does your product meet that need in a manner that either saves or makes you substantial amounts of money? For example, I love hot pepper jelly. It is a wonderful glaze when melted over grilled salmon, but I hate to make it

even though I know how. So, I purchase a 4-ounce jar for $3.99 every two or three months. I would purchase a case if I could. What does that tell me?

Now that you have these three "big picture" questions in mind, you can start to think about the specific questions that you would like to ask your potential customers. Normally you come up with a set of questions that help you to understand how the audience is thinking and feeling about your product. The goal is to gain intimate knowledge of your customers. You want to know exactly what they are thinking and feeling, and why.

How to Write an E-marketing Plan

An e-marketing plan is used to achieve profitable sales similar to a traditional marketing plan, except the scope is limited to online and offline advertising digital technologies to help sell your products. These technologies may include article marketing, promotions using e-mail and social media, and paid search campaigns. Though businesses will continue to make use of traditional marketing methods, such as advertising, direct mail, and public relations, e-marketing adds a whole new element to the marketing mix. Many businesses are producing great results with e-marketing and its flexible and cost-effective nature makes it particularly suitable for small businesses. If you would like to learn more about e-marketing plans, there is a wonderful book titled *Turn Your Online Marketing Around: The Complete Reference to Web 2.0 Marketing and Advertising Tools* by Claudie Clot.

E-marketing plans are separate from traditional business plans and address those sales and marketing goals that will brand your business and build a buzz around your product, thereby promoting sales and exposure. Components of an e-marketing plan may include the following:

- Executive Summary
- Company Overview
- Target Markets
- Demographic Research
- Online Advertising
- Online Promotions
- Offline Advertising
- Offline Promotions

Executive Summary

The document you are writing is for you, and although you may share it with business partners and others, it should be used to assist you in marketing your home-based bakery business. Your executive summary is presented first, yet it is written after the entire marketing plan has been completed. It should not contain any information that cannot be found elsewhere in the business plan. The following is a sample Executive Summary for a small home-based cookie bakery.

Bailey's Cookie Basket is an online retailer offering unique decorated cookies in beautifully made custom boxes. Based on the research conducted on e-commerce purchasing trends and the browsing trends of similar food-based Web sites, we expect our main demographic to be women between the ages of 25 and 54 years.

This marketing plan will cover our online and offline advertising and promotions and will highlight the ways by which we will go about carrying out each campaign. Our online promotions and advertising campaigns will direct traffic to our Web site and highlight and promote our brand. Online promotions and advertisements include paid search campaigns, media buying campaigns, and e-newsletters directed at previous and potential customers.

Our offline promotions and advertising campaigns will direct traffic to our Web site and highlight and promote our brand as well. Offline promotions and advertisements include product donations to public television auctions, public/private school fund-raising initiatives, specialized vehicle designs, advertising space in magazines frequented by our target demographic, product tasting at farmer's markets and gourmet stores, and "refer-a-friend" discount purchase coupons distributed with shipments.

Company Overview

The company overview is a summation of all the products and services the company will offer over the course of the marketing campaign.

Target Markets

Your target market will be made up of a group of potential customers whose needs and preferences match the product range of your company and to whom those products are marketed. You may want to use online focus groups as opposed to in-person focus groups in order to validate the integrity of your data. By conducting an online focus group, you will be able to study individuals from various parts of your community and demonstrate animated advertisements and Web site functions to see what is most effective in promoting a response.

Demographic Research

If you are interested in doing your own demographic research, consider using www .freedemographics.com, which may provide information on the shopping habits of those individuals in your community who may need your products and services.

Online Advertising and Online Promotions

This may involve running various media campaigns of interactive and flash adver-tisements—e.g., the creation of a Ning.com Web site, an online network that allows food processors to create their own social networks, thereby providing information to potential customers.

Offline Advertising and Offline Promotions

This could be a magnetic sign for the side of your car or even a personalized license plate. Other offline promotions may involve partnering with a nonprofit agency or sponsoring a product tasting.

This type of marketing plan may appear a bit involved, and in some cases you might not need to address all of the areas described, but you should address at least some of the strategies discussed and participate in a bit of demographic research to learn who your specific customers are and where they are located.

Consider a Press Release

A news release, media release, press release, or press statement is a written or recorded communication directed at members of the news media for the purpose of announcing something of newsworthy value.

Ask yourself, "Would the announcement of my new home-based bakery be newsworthy?" Remember, there will be times when your news will be competing with major news stories. Then ask yourself, "After writing my press release, to whom should I send it and why?"

Let's get the "why" out the way first. A press release is different from a news article. A news article is a compilation of facts developed by journalists published in the news media, whereas a press release is designed to be sent to journalists in order to encourage them to develop articles on a subject. You want someone, namely a reporter, to write an article about your new business. A press release is generally biased towards the objectives of the author, so you need to write it either yourself or in conjunction with a good writing assistant. A press release is written in order to highlight an important event, program, or piece of information by an organization, and it succinctly describes the who, what, where, when, why, and how of a story.

Who?	Who are you, what's your name, and share a bit about yourself.
What?	Your home-based bakery.
Where?	Where is your home-based bakery, or where are your goods sold in the community?
When?	When will your goods and services be available?
Why?	Why did you start this business, and how will the community benefit from it?
How?	How can customers locate you for more information?

Not everyone should receive your press releases; not everyone will read them. Five well-targeted recipients of press releases will be much more effective than one hundred randomly sent ones. While press releases sent over online wire services like Business Wire or PR News Wire may reach a wide range of media outlets, it can be equally effective to target specific publications and even specific journalists. I do not suggest you use any type of Business Wire or PR News Wire unless you are selling your product online and want to reach a nationwide audience.

Typically, the larger and more general the publication, the bigger your story must be to get coverage. If you are a small but growing startup home bakery, you have a better chance of coverage or a profile in the community newspaper or a local/regional magazine. Press releases should be sent to a specific person, usually the reporter most likely to write a story about your bakery, for example a food writer or community news writer.

Once you have identified the correct recipients of your press release, make sure that your writing is up to snuff and that you include all of the necessary information. You may not have the time or the expertise to craft ideal press releases. If that's the

12 Steps to a Great Press Release

A press release is considered by some to be an old-fashioned way to introduce a new business, product, or service. They have been around for years, and they are still frequently used by companies large and small. The primary difference today is that they can be mailed, e-mailed, posted on message boards, placed in online newspapers—the sky's the limit. The biggest challenge, however, is getting the right folks to read it.

Another important thing you need to know about a press release is that it is not an advertisement. While a successful press release can help your company acquire new customers, its primary purpose is to spread the word about your news story. Here are twelve steps to creating a great press release:

1. Make sure the information is newsworthy.
2. Ask yourself, "How are people going to relate to this and will they be able to connect?"
3. Make sure the first ten words of your release are effective, as they are the most important.
4. Start with a brief description of the news; then distinguish who announced it, and not the other way around.
5. Tell the reader that the information is intended for them and why they should continue to read it.
6. Avoid excessive use of adjectives and colorful language.
7. Deal with the facts.
8. Provide as much contact information as possible: individual to contact, address, phone, fax, e-mail, Web site address.
9. Make sure you wait until you have something with enough substance to issue a release.
10. Make it as easy as possible for media representatives to do their jobs.
11. Provide a head shot. Media representatives like to put a face to the product/ service.
12. Send your release electronically as an attachment and/or in the body of the e-mail.

case, consider hiring a consultant to write your press release, or ask a friend who is a gifted writer. You can always repay them with some fine baked goods!

Here is a sample press release for a home-based baker:

For Immediate Release
January 1, 2011
[Name of your company] PRESENTS
. . . [your tag line]!
[Your city and state]—January 1, 2011—(Your Company Name) announces its grand opening to (XXX) residents. The bakery will be taking orders for holiday cookies beginning November 17, 2010, by phone, e-mail, and at our new location.

The XXXXX Bakery recently set up camp at the Wall Town Farmer's Market. Jane Doe will be selling her famous gourmet cookies every Wednesday and Saturday at the market between 10:00 a.m. and 6:00 p.m.

Jane has been baking for friends and neighbors for more than ten years and decided this holiday she would offer her delectable sweet treats to her community. She is thrilled to be a feature baker at the ever growing and robust Wall Town Farmer's Market.

The XXXXX Bakery is committed to offering great tasting, quality cookies along with Jane's special Whole Grain Buttermilk Bread, and the ever popular No Life without Dark Chocolate Brownies. This year the XXXXX Bakery is featuring a Cookie Christmas Tree fashioned along the lines of a gingerbread house. The Christmas tree ornaments are made up of a variety of intricately decorated miniature sugar cookies. It is truly a sight to behold.

The XXXXX Bakery specializes in creating signature cookies for local organizations and will design a special corporate gift idea for your company. Wall Town residents are invited to visit Jane at the Wall Town Farmer's Market, or visit www.thexxxxxbakery.com for more information about products and services.

About The XXXXX Bakery
Jane Doe bakes and serves fresh-baked cookies and breads. She designs beautiful signature cookies for anyone looking for a unique and delicious

food gift. The XXXXX Bakery is a home-based bakery committed to using great-tasting, quality ingredients and contributing to the neighborhoods in which our customers live and work through contributions to the local food banks and donations to the Children's Hospital Annual Fundraising Event. For more information about The XXXXX Bakery visit www. thexxxxxbakery.com. Don't forget to ask about our new Cookie Christmas Tree, the perfect holiday gift!

Contact:
Jane Doe
The XXXXX Bakery
P O Box 5555
Wall Town, Virginia 27701
276-551-5555
www.thexxxxxbakery.com
###

Word-of-Mouth Advertising

The impact of the Internet has caused word-of-mouth marketing to take on a whole new meaning and has changed buyer behavior and purchasing power. It compels customers to spread the word about your products faster than they would have been able to ten years ago. Information about your product can span the globe in a matter of minutes and in some cases seconds. Learning about your products is literally just a mouse click or text message away.

No longer is word-of-mouth advertising tied to a telephone call; social networking and multimedia strategies now allow you to tell customers and potential customers about your products as soon as they come out of the test kitchen.

Today word-of-mouth advertising is important for every business, and it is becoming one of the most credible forms of advertising because people put their reputation on the line every time they recommend your product.

Ask yourself, "What am I doing to generate a positive word-of-mouth buzz for my chocolate chunk brownies or my double fudge chocolate chip cookies?" One of the primary ways to encourage a positive buzz about your product is to provide your customers with something that far exceeds what they expected. Going above and beyond anything they might anticipate is a surefire way to get folks talking.

The Truth about Social Media and Social Networking

A loose definition of a social networking group is a collection of people interconnected either directly or indirectly who interact with or influence one another. Today there are social networking groups surrounding every business, organization, and individual, and it doesn't matter if they are well known to the general public.

It is your responsibility as a new small business owner to build a social networking group around your company, one that is interested in what you have to offer. How you create a collective group of people committed to your product depends not only on how social media savvy you are but also on how adept you are at using and creating Web pages that are committed to sharing information about your new bakery business.

Some of the more popular social media Web sites include:

Bebo: www.bebo.com

Facebook: www.facebook.com

FastPitch!: www.fastpitchnetworking.com

Friendster: www.friendster.com

Gather.com: www.gather.com

LinkedIn: www.linkedin.com

MySpace: www.myspace.com

Moli: www.moli.com

Ning: www.ning.com

Orkut: www.orkut.com

There are going to be times when it will be advantageous to be involved in some form of social networking. Your home-based bakery will not fail if you do not have a Facebook page or if you are not on LinkedIn; but know that these networking platforms have had a tremendous impact on how people discover, read, and share news about what is going on in their world.

One of the best uses of social networking by a home-based baker is by Andrea Bigelow, owner of Yummy to Your Tummy, Desserts by Andrea. This home-based baker has learned to use her Facebook page to not only spread the word about her home-based bakery, but she also introduces new "members of my family," what she affectionately calls the new baked goods she sells to her customers. Andrea is committed to staying in front of her Facebook fans and sharing all her baking experiences with her customers while attracting new patrons to her page at the same time. It is through social networking that you will form a unique relationship with your customers, and they will come to learn about you, your business, your products, and your commitment to making quality baked goods. (For more information on social networking, see Chapters 7 and 9).

Keeping Track of Your Customers

There are few things more important in business than keeping track of current and former customers. Most large businesses have always kept customer information on file using database systems; however, today it is becoming easier for small businesses to keep databases allowing them to track customer activity and preferences.

Putting together a database system can be expensive for the average home-based baker; an alternative would be to maintain a simple Excel spreadsheet or consider an e-mail marketing service like the following:

- iContact
- Constant Contact
- Easy Contact
- Vertical Response

What I like about these services is that they allow you to post specific comments about the customer, e.g., *loves chocolate candy and truffles* or *is partial to cupcakes and miniature desserts*. This allows you the opportunity to e-mail specials to those customers who will want what you have to offer.

While many customers are concerned about private information being kept in company databases, as a home-based baker using one of these e-mail marketing services, you offer your customers the opportunity to receive mailings and be contacted regarding specific products that are of interest to them rather than receiving blanket mailings about a variety of products that they do not want.

It is recommended that you keep the documentation of each specific customer's likes and dislikes to a minimum if at all possible; and remember that this information is for your use only and should never be given or sold to any third party entity.

Even though you are a small business, as a customer-oriented business, it makes good business sense to adhere to the highest standards in regard to making sure your customer's information is being collected with the utmost privacy standards and maintained in a secure environment.

If you are accepting checks or cash, you may want to keep a record of how much someone spends on each order; however, you may not want to keep a copy of the actual check since that allows you to have access to bank routing numbers and checking account numbers, information you do not really need.

It is best to maintain records on only the basic information needed to complete your sales transactions. Some home-based bakers also use automated payment systems like PayPal, an e-commerce business that allows payments and money transfers to be made through the Internet. In this way the e-commerce payment service maintains all credit or payment information and, although there are fees associated with this payment function, you do not have to bother with maintaining payment records or sensitive information. There are many e-commerce payment services available, and all have varying fees for service, so it is best to shop around for the service that best suits your needs.

Bookkeeping and Management

Bookkeeping is the process of keeping full, accurate, up-to-date business records. The methods used by home-based bakers to effectively manage cash flow and stay abreast of profits and losses is probably different for every baker. Some bakers use a simple spreadsheet while others use bookkeeping software, and still others have a certified public account address their financial gains and losses. In addition to measuring the financial health of the business, this information is also essential for addressing both federal and local tax responsibilities.

The amount of financial work for a home-based baker will depend on the amount of baking done and the amount of money spent and earned. I learned the hard way that paperwork can pile up quickly, and during your heavy baking seasons you may not have time to address those bookkeeping needs like you want, so you should seriously consider working with an accountant.

The operation of your home-based bakery should be professional and allow you to access information easily. The biggest challenge will be taking time to review your finances each day. I have found it best to set aside about thirty minutes a day to review all bills and other financial obligations, then additionally set aside about two hours a week to pay bills, address vendor inquires, pay taxes, and address any other business needs.

Depending on where you live, there may be special taxes you must pay. For example, in the state of North Carolina, there is a bread tax that must be paid. It is the responsibility of each home-based baker to investigate and learn about any special taxes you will incur. Don't fool yourself into thinking that, because you have no knowledge of a certain tax, you don't have to pay it.

Keeping track of your finances will pay off each time state, federal, and other taxes come due. Having all your paperwork in order benefits both you and your accountant, preventing the two of you from potentially having to sift through mounds of paperwork and receipts.

Seeking Professional Assistance

It may not appear to be relevant now because you are just starting your home-based bakery business, but at some point you will need to seek professional assistance with your bookkeeping needs; or if you are currently using an accounting system, you may outgrow it as your business grows and becomes more complex. It doesn't matter if you use a manual ledger, an Excel spreadsheet, or a lockbox—the financial responsibilities associated with your home-based bakery will generate lots of receipts, and you will need to track customer billing, tax payments, and other financial obligations.

When operating a small business, there is always a balance that must be struck between time and money. You need to analyze how much time you spend on baking and how much time you spend on financial issues. One thing is certain: If you do not address your financial matters regularly and accurately, the cost to your business (and to you) may be severe. For example, if you decide to buy the least-expensive accounting program that you can find on the shelf of your local office supply store, you may spend an extra 20 hours per week trying to figure out if it will do what you need it to do. If you could take that 20 hours and sell more cakes, pies, and cookies to your customers, then perhaps it would be worth spending more on a bookkeeping program that can provide you with all of the services you need in a quick and convenient fashion.

When seeking bookkeeping software for your home-based business your key concern should be:

- Price of the software
- Ease of implementation
- Ease of use
- Technical Support

You want a program that offers a level of support that is turn-key ready; in other words, you want to load the software easily and be up and running quickly. Unfortunately, it's never quite that simple, so pay close attention to the type and amount of support services offered by the software company. It's imperative that you can easily and economically access customer and technical support for your new system.

Vehicle Mileage Documentation

Home-based bakers who deliver their goods to customers may be able to deduct the cost of operating their car for business purposes. For more information visit the Internal Revenue Service Web page at www.irs.gov/newsroom/article/0,,id=216048,00.html. The current mileage rate for 2010 is 50 cents per mile for business miles driven. This rate is subject to change annually so bakers should check the IRS Web site every year for new mileage rates.

Vehicle Mileage Log

Date/For the week of:_____

Date	Odometer Reading		Miles Traveled	Purpose/ Destination	Total Miles
	Start	End			
Total Mileage					

There are bookkeeping software companies that charge for technical support calls, which is fine as long as you are able to speak to a live person. You will also want to know whether there are consultants based locally that can come to your home and provide customized setup and training, if needed.

Remember that bookkeeping software is generally updated annually, so there are many opportunities for programming errors to arise; pay close attention to the number of years a company has been in business and be wary of open source or free software programs that make claims they are as good as, or better than, those programs in the office stores that are more costly.

If you are going to use a bookkeeping software program, make sure it fits your business and avoid any one-size-fits-all types of programs. Some programs will allow you to customize various parts of the program, and others allow you to maintain inventory and/or track billable time. Having a good understanding of what's most important for your business's financial needs is essential. If you don't need bells and whistles in a software program, don't buy them.

One small business bookkeeping software, Intuit QuickBooks, tracks every dollar that comes into and goes out of your business. It also instantly creates invoices, tracks payments, and manages your expenses. You can also try checking with your local bank to see if they have free bookkeeping software associated with your small business checking account that will assist you in tracking your financial needs.

Learning about Specialty Food Taxes

When discussing what taxes you will pay as a home-based baker, things can get a bit confusing with state sales tax rates. For example, I lived in North Carolina where there was a huge controversy over whether or not bakers would pay the assigned 2 percent tax as opposed to the prepared-food tax of 7.75 percent. The debate was whether or not bakery products should be classified as a "prepared food," which is defined as food that is sold hot or heated by the retailer, mixed or combined by the retailer, or sold with eating utensils provided by the retailer.

The North Carolina Department of Revenue representatives seemed to be telling the taxpayers one thing but requesting an alternative tax rate from bakers; and after years of legislative debates, the Small Business Tax Protection Act passed and the sales tax paid by bakers was reduced to 2 percent.

Lesson learned: Check with your state department of revenue to make sure you are paying any and all state sales taxes, and get the requirements in writing.

There are no states that are completely tax free. However, in some states, the tax burden is considerably less than in others. According to information gathered by the United States Census, sales taxes overall account for approximately 25 percent of the money needed to run state and local governments. Money collected via sales taxes is used to provide essential services, such as education, police, and fire protection. So it is imperative that you find out exactly which sales tax you will have to collect from your customers and pay to the government. Don't take for granted that just because you are selling beautifully decorated cookies that you do not have to pay taxes. You do.

Federal Taxes for the Self-Employed

Running a home-based bakery implies that you are self-employed if you are charging money for your baked goods. The Internal Revenue Service has set forth appropriate guidelines when determining whether an activity is for profit, such as a home-based bakery business, or a hobby.

Internal Revenue Code Section 183 (Activities Not Engaged in for Profit) limits the amount of deductions that can be claimed when an activity is not engaged in for profit; sometimes referred to as the "hobby loss rule."

You may want to talk to your accountant to make sure you have a clear understanding of what constitutes a "for-profit" activity and the tax implications for incorrectly treating a hobby as a for-profit activity.

The federal government allows taxpayers to deduct ordinary and necessary expenses for conducting a trade or business or for the production of income. Your home-based baking business activities and those performed for the production of income are considered activities engaged in for profit.

The following factors, although not all-inclusive, may help you to determine whether your activity is an activity engaged in for profit or a hobby:

- Does the time and effort put into baking indicate an intention to make a profit?
- Do you depend on income from your home bakery business?
- If there are losses, are they due to circumstances beyond your control, or did they occur in the start-up phase of your bakery business?
- Do you have the knowledge needed to carry on the activity as a successful business?

- Have you made a profit in similar activities in the past?
- Does the activity make a profit in some years?
- Do you expect to make a profit in the future from the appreciation of assets used in the activity?

Your home-based bakery is presumed to be a for-profit business if it makes a profit in at least three of the last five tax years, including the current year. If you have specific questions, consult an accountant, a financial expert, or visit www.irs .gov/localcontacts/index.html.

Managing a Home Bakery Business

Managing a home-based bakery is no more complex than managing any other home-based business. There are times when time management and family responsibilities will interfere with your role as a baker; and without stern commitment to creating a clear separation between work and family, you might find yourself frustrated and stressed.

Managing two responsibilities in one space is difficult for anyone. This is why strategizing how you will manage your home bakery and family needs is vital. A little disorganization or some poorly planned days can cost you a substantial amount of time and money.

Plan Your Day

As a home-based baker, it is imperative that you plan your baking days as far ahead as possible. Do not worry about listing all baking preparation responsibilities with a time period just yet; start first to make a list and assess what needs to be completed each morning for your bakery.

For example, every morning I would:

- Check my e-mails for orders
- Listen to my voice mail for inquiries
- Check my calendar for daily orders

After assessing the morning inquiries, I would make a list of what needed to be completed that day and prioritize the list. Looking at the delivery times would dictate when I would bake or complete a baked good and get it either mailed or delivered.

There is no real right or wrong way to manage your business; there is only an efficient or more efficient way to manage things. You must pay attention to the little things and know that there will always be smaller tasks that don't get finished at the end of the day or week. Don't beat yourself up if you do not crush all the graham crackers for next week's pie order or store that newly arrived case of boxes in the closet. There are times when you won't be able to do much as you would like; just relax, try not to let it accumulate to the point that it prevents you from doing important things, and if you really get in a pickle, ask for help from family or friends.

Make Room for Downtime

Starting a home-based bakery does not necessarily mean you need to purchase a BlackBerry, buy a fancy laptop computer, or run out and hire a receptionist. A cell phone is a great tool along with the know-how to use those phone features that will allow you to keep communications open with both your customers and family. There are some bakers who use a daily planner and others who just maintain a notebook to jot down information they need to remember.

Outsourcing Your Responsibilities

There may be a time when you need to outsource specific responsibilities, for example, advertising, delivery of specific products, marketing, and those family commitments like picking up the kids from school or dropping them off at the soccer field. You may also need to outsource the laundry or house cleaning, although this is where family members may need to step up and assist.

Have you figured out how much money you can make in an hour? Divide your monthly income by the actual hours worked. This does not mean the hours spent in the office talking to potential customers or the hours sitting at the computer checking e-mails; it means the actual hours you are actively engaging in earning revenue on actual baking projects.

Once you know what kind of revenue you are pulling in, calculate how much time you will spend taking out the trash, doing the laundry and house work, and picking up the boys from soccer. These responsibilities may take 18 hours a week. A business owner may earn $25 an hour yet end up losing $450 a week because he or she will not delegate some of the mundane household tasks to another family member.

Home vs. Work

Home-based bakers need to remember that baking takes time, sometime lots of time. There are many stages involved in preparing baked goods, so plan accordingly. To manage your time efficiently, decide which hours are to be invested in work, and which belong to your home life. Sit down with your family and teach them about what this new home bakery business will mean to the family as a whole.

Explain there may be times when you do not want to be disturbed until you are finished working. There will also be times when family members will have to fend for themselves because you are delivering products, meeting with a customer, or addressing online or telephone inquiries. Everything you put into place is a plan of action that will help you succeed and help you learn how to manage your business successfully.

Caring for Your Children

Managing a successful home-based bakery business around your children is a difficult task. It may take a bit more than just following strict time schedules, since there may be times when your child may need your loving care and attention, particularly when he or she isn't feeling well. In such situations, you will need to adjust your schedule to suit your child's needs. As you create a daily plan, think about what you would do if you had a family emergency and had to tend to an ailing child all while attempting to put the finishing touches on a dessert buffet for one hundred guests.

The thought may pop into your mind that this is part of the reason you are working at home—to spend time with your children; but remember, you have business responsibilities that you must fulfill if you want to maintain customer support and satisfaction.

If you have older children, you can lay down ground rules that keep them informed about what you need from them in order to operate your business effectively; it is by establishing appropriate rules that you often provide yourself with a clear path for completing tasks and laying the groundwork for teaching your children how to pitch in and take on those responsibilities that not only benefit you but the whole household.

Having your older children assist you in your home-based bakery business as they grow older helps them become instrumental in building the company and teaches them about how to operate a home-based business. After school, your children can be helpful in more ways than you realize. Giving them work they can manage, e.g., take out trash, walk the dog, set the dinner table, fold clothes, will help you as well, allowing you to be with your children and work at the same time.

Managing Your Cost

The cost of operating a home-based business can be considerably less than renting an office and incurring the expenses associated with a brick-and-mortar location; however, while your costs are much lower in some areas, there is still a need to manage these costs to ensure that your business remains profitable.

The expense of operating a home-based bakery business involves both fixed overhead costs and variable costs, all linked to the production of the baked goods you provide your customers. It is these fundamental areas that you must focus on and adequately manage to ensure you have a profitable home-based baking business.

Fixed overhead costs are expenses that occur every month regardless of whether you sell any baked goods. They include such things as utilities, rent, taxes, and any other costs that are going to occur regardless of the amount of revenue you take in; these costs need to be managed closely, since once you commit to any increases in such costs, that change can impact your bottom line.

Variable costs are directly related to your production of goods. Think of it this way: As production goes up, so do your costs for labor, raw materials, packaging, shipping, and support. The per-unit cost of your product should be monitored closely to make sure that as your volume increases, you gain efficiencies, which drives your per-unit cost down and your profit up.

Cost of sales are costs that are directly related to the activity of selling to your customers, for example running online ads, making and distributing brochures, etc. Management of these costs is very important and should be directly related to securing additional business. Pay close attention to these costs to ensure that your business remains profitable even as you are adding new markets or new products that may again impact your bottom line.

Isolation

Most home-based bakers initially think that working from home is a breeze and the perfect way to take care of family needs, all while doing something they love; and making extra income. Oftentimes bakers think working from home brings about some obvious benefits, such as setting your own hours; avoiding a stressful, tedious commute; not having to answer to a boss; being home when your children return from school; and working in a comfortable, familiar environment. It's true these are some of the creature comforts of operating a home-based business, but it is not all sugar and spice.

Once your home-based bakery is up and running and the telephone starts ringing, you will discover that sometimes not being in a traditional work environment means there is no stopping to chat with coworkers or time to take a leisurely walk to the cafeteria for a snack or even a walk around the company grounds after lunch. There are no drinks after work on Friday night or team-building sessions to solidify work-team camaraderie. Before long, you may begin to think back to your previous life and realize you actually miss those umpteen coworkers who were constantly interrupting you when you were trying to work, the walk in the park at lunchtime with your best work-friend, or meeting up with a colleague for dinner after work.

As a home-based businessperson, you must make every effort to avoid the isolation trap and structure your workday in such a manner that you balance your day with a variety of activities. You really don't want to start your workday without a plan; so arrange a specified work time, lunch, office time, and if possible, squeeze in some exercise or a daily walk, even if it involves walking down the street to chat with a neighbor for fifteen to twenty minutes. If possible, structure your time so that it is not an endless day of baking with no time for outside human interaction.

Social Networking

Social networking is a vital skill and part of operating a home-based bakery business. It is important that you make contacts with people who can add value to your business, as well as connect with other small business owners in the outside world.

Some of us have gone from sending work correspondence via "snail mail" to telephones and now to e-mail and text messages. Today you have computers, handheld devices, and so much more at your disposal. If you need to contact a bride about the topper on her wedding cake, you can call her on a land line or cellphone, or e-mail, text and, if needed, send a photo via any one of these communication formats.

Social networking is a superior way to report news about your business to your customers faster than any other medium. Many home-based bakers also have blogs that provide information about their products and services and new trends that are circulating the country. For example, if you specialize in gluten-free breads, you may want to blog about the gluten-free movement and educate Web site visitors about why gluten-free products are important to the population.

Joining a professional group or club and attending workshops and trade shows relevant to baking and small food processing are great ways to meet new people who have similar interests and challenges. It is important to participate in these activities and take a good supply of business cards with you.

There are most likely a number of workshops and training seminars sponsored by the Small Business Administration in your community. Visit www.sba.gov/local resources/index.html to locate the SBA office in your area.

Ning.com is the social networking Web site that brings people from all over the world together to explore and express their interests, discover new passions, and meet new people around shared pursuits. Check out Food Entrepreneurs at http://specialtyfood.ning.com/ to learn about specialty food marketing.

Meetup.com is a large network of local groups organized to help you locate others who share your interests. You may want to start your own Meetup.com group of home-based bakers, or you may want to join a small business group to gain ideas about advertising and marketing your products. Visit www.meetup.com/ to learn more.

Use the Internet

If by some chance you are not familiar with how to use the Internet and surf the web, *learn*. Making friends online is a great way to not only stay connected with the outside world, but it is a wonderful way to learn more about the home-based baking industry and learn how to resolve issues that might arise. I have a Web site called Cooking with Denay (http://cookingwithdenay.com/) that offers information and resources for home-based bakers.

There are countless baking sites and message boards that will assist you in troubleshooting baking issues and locating products and hard-to-find ingredients. Making online friends is another way of staying connected with the outside world, but you must exhibit restraint; spending large amounts of time on the Internet can prevent you from completing your daily work. Stay focused.

How do you come up with a great recipe? Well, a great recipe is simply one that you love; one that has a delicious taste and is not too costly to reproduce. It might be grandma's secret recipe handed down through the years or a modification of a recipe that you find in a Betty Crocker cookbook—you know, the one that friends plead with you to share. It might be for a cake, a sauce, or that awesome Christmas candy made once a year and given as gifts to friends and family.

I know a number of bakers and home food processors who search the Internet for recipes; but recipes found on the Internet, like all others, must be tested and sampled before sold. There is no foolproof recipe, and there are countless variables that go into ensuring that a recipe is consistent time and time again.

For example I use a particular brand of vanilla that comes from a company in New Orleans. When Hurricane Katrina hit, the company was out of business for a while, and I was unable to procure my secret ingredient. By the time they were up and running again, I was in a full panic. The lesson I learned from that experience: Make sure you use products that are easily accessible and that can be substituted.

Culture also determines a good recipe. If you are fortunate enough to have a recipe that is a cultural favorite and something new to the general public, go for it. Just remember that everyone's taste buds are different, and the flavors that entice one culture may be less appealing to another, so make sure you do a bit of market research first.

In our fast-paced society, we don't usually spend as much time in the kitchen whipping up those great recipes as our grandparents once did in days gone by. A good recipe is simply defined by what you like and enjoy. A good recipe is the one that's a hit at every get-together. A good recipe is the one that your friends are begging you to give them. A good recipe is what you make of it! And if you are going to use this wonderful recipe to create baked goods for sale, remember to share it with no one. Keep it under lock and key, if necessary.

You should try pairing familiar ingredients that you don't usually put together; for example, flavor a pear pie with a hint of ginger. Or try borrowing the key flavors of one dish and incorporating them into a different form. For instance, a plain oatmeal cookie recipe could be combined with pecans, prunes, raisins, or cran-raisins; spread on a cookie sheet; and reinterpreted as a breakfast bar made with oatmeal and dried fruits.

Go to the grocery store and wander through sections that you don't usually visit. Look on the top and bottom shelves for unusual or imported items. These explorations and experiments can launch you in new culinary directions.

Take inspiration from your favorite restaurant. Order a dessert you would not normally select and think about what you could do to make it more pleasing to the taste buds. Write down a few notes to help you remember.

Study recipes that are similar to what you want to create. If you want to make a different type of muffin, there's no need to reinvent the whole thing. Baking is chemistry, and there is a finite number of flour, leavening, and liquid combinations that will work. Find one or two reliable models and study them to determine how they might be tweaked.

Before you begin baking, create a style sheet for your version of the recipe. As you prepare it and as you taste it, keep your pen handy. Make notes and alter proportions as necessary.

Test the recipe at least three times. Occasionally, you'll get lucky and score perfection on the first try, but more often you'll want another pass at it.

Try to judge the dish objectively. Ask yourself questions as you sample it. Is it too sweet? Too heavy? Does it need more salt or chocolate or vanilla? Ask other people to taste it and solicit their opinions.

A Home Bakery Checklist

The following checklist provides details of what you need in order to develop your products. Factors that may affect what you decide to bake and sell include the target market, number of people to be served, available equipment, amount of labor involved in producing the product, and the cost of processing.

The recipe development checklist is a tool to assist you in the creation of new recipes and ensures that you have provided all the information necessary to make a consistently perfect baked good every time. Your first thought may be that you do not need to go through all of this trouble for one chocolate chip cookie recipe. But if you are selling to the public, you want to know that the cookie will come out perfectly every time you bake it; and this is a great way to ensure consistency. It really is best to leave nothing to chance, since your customers will not understand when the cookies they purchase are void of salt or vanilla flavor because you inadvertently forgot to put them into that particular batch.

Scaling Recipes

If you choose to scale a recipe (double or triple it), don't adjust the oven temperature to compensate for the increased volume unless you are prepared to throw out a lot of batches that don't turn out right. Some bakers claim you should reduce the oven temperature when baking a certain recipe in a larger pan than normally used. In general, I don't recommend it because it is a fairly complex decision, based upon a lot of variables. In general the larger the surface area that's exposed to the heat, the faster a cake will bake. There are a number of great books on cake baking. *The Cake Bible* by Rose Levy Beranbaum is a wonderful book for cake bakers. Check out her Web site at www.realbakingwithrose.com/, which is also a great resource for any baker.

Organizing Your Baking Time

The one lesson I learned quickly as a home-based baker is that timing is everything. It is one thing to bake for your family, who pays little to no attention if the brownies are not ready right after dinner; it is completely different to bake for a customer who is counting on your baking and delivering five dozen brownies for a birthday celebration that starts at 1:00 p.m. on a Saturday afternoon, and will be attended by twenty-nine hungry eight-year-olds.

If you are baking more than one item for more than one event on the same day, organize your time and pay close attention to which products can be left to stand for

Recipe Development Checklist

Each time you create a new recipe, use this checklist to ensure you have written the recipe properly.

Recipe Name:	Yes	No
Does the recipe give a sufficient description of the major ingredient or preparation?		
Is the recipe name appealing?		
Have you listed all of the ingredients in the recipe?		
Are the ingredients listed in the order in which they are used?		
Are the measurements given in common fractions (e.g., ½ cup, ¼ cup, etc.)?		
Are the ingredients listed in the easiest unit of measure (e.g., ¼ cup instead of 4 tablespoons)?		
Are all measurements spelled out, not abbreviated (e.g., cup, teaspoon)?		
Are container sizes specified (e.g., 4-ounce can, 12-ounce bag)?		
Are brand names avoided (e.g., Hershey's Chocolate)? There is no way to guarantee brand name products will always be available so whenever possible use a high quality generic brand.		
Are ingredients listed with complete descriptions (e.g., low fat, packed in syrup) and with the exact type of product specified (e.g., cake flour, all-purpose flour, dark brown sugar, etc.)?		
Are the sizes of the pans or containers stated in the recipe (e.g., 9 x 2½-inch nonstick round layer pans)?		
Are the temperatures given for recipes requiring the oven?		
Are all cooking and/or baking times and preparation times stated?		
Are the number and size of servings included in the recipe?		

a few hours and which cannot. If you are baking two pound cakes and eight dozen cookies, you may want to get the pound cakes completed first, allowing them time to season before you deliver, then save the cookies for last, since homemade cookies only stay fresh for one to two days and are best eaten the same day they are baked.

Home-based baking can be a bit more challenging than initially anticipated if you do not organize your time and pay close attention to the needs of the products and your customers. There will be some customers who will want a product hot out of the oven. This is often unrealistic, and you should never promise something you cannot deliver. One alternative I offered years ago was going to the clients' homes and preparing the desserts. It was more time consuming and costly to the customers, but they had fresh, hot baked goods for their special events. My fee was $25 per hour, plus the cost of ingredients and any special requests. This request was not made often, but when I could accommodate a customer, I did, leaving them with the memory of wonderful baked goods that made their home smell heavenly.

Along with timing, it is also difficult to predict how much of an ingredient you should have on hand until you actually begin operating your business. You will need to decide first whom you will sell to and what your introductory market base will be. For example, if you are selling to friends and family, what will your turnaround time be? If they order on Monday, can you supply the product by Wednesday? Thursday? Or can you handle next-day pick-up and/or delivery?

Start slow and have enough ingredients, packaging, and supplies on hand to address the needs of a minimal number of orders until you develop a feel for your workflow capabilities. This is why it is important to select a launch date or select a date when you will be showcasing your baked goods. It is far better to run out and obtain contact information to build a waiting list than to be left with goods that did not sell.

Developing a Product Line

A mistake commonly made by home-based bakers just starting out is the overwhelming desire to bake everything under the sun. My advice is to specialize in one or two baked goods and then get creative by combining popular products that aren't normally paired together, such as gluten-free cookies and breads or no bake cookies and dried fruit bars. What's important is that you give customers the impression that you've "got it all together," and you are not just baking as a hobbyist who can't decide what to sell. Focus is important.

Contracts

Every baker needs to develop a contract for special baking assignments. Write the contract in simple language that both parties can understand, and state the terms of the agreement. Seek the advice of an attorney for any particularly large job or for anything about which you are uncertain. Be sure to include the following elements in each of your written contracts:

Names, addresses, and telephone numbers of parties involved (buyer and seller)
Date of the agreement and date of the event/delivery
Time of event/delivery
Location of event/delivery
Product setup, baskets, decorations, tablecloths, etc., to be used
Types of products
Estimated and guaranteed number of products sold
Service arrangements
Pricing arrangements and potential price increases
Deposit required (25, 30, or 50 percent of cost when the contract is signed)
Discount (if any) for full payment at the time contract is signed
Cancellation provisions specifying cases of cancellation because of illness, broken engagement, or death. (The contract needs to specify how much of the deposit will be retained in the event of a cancellation.)
Applicable taxes
Include space for signatures at the bottom of the contract form

Carefully consider contract terms, write them in simple language, and print them in a size that is easy to read. This is to ensure that everyone understands the terms of the contract.

Students in my online classes, when asked what their signature product is, often mention pound cake, cheesecake, brownies, cookies, *and* granola bars. This is when I must bring them down to earth and ask, "So will you have all the ingredients on hand for those products regardless of whether or not someone requests the products?" Many home-based bakers have not given enough thought to the amount of ingredients and supplies needed to prepare all such products, should a customer ask for two, three, or more of them in considerable quantities at the same time.

While it's important to focus on a signature product you love and are good at baking, you must also consider the marketplace. Baking what you love to bake is not necessarily going to be what people want to buy, so you must do some market research before you begin to develop your product line. For example if you love to make pound cakes, but most of your customers are cutting back on calories and want smaller versions of this product, consider making miniature pound cakes and selling them in twin gift boxes. In this way, the customer can keep buying from you and consider giving one to a family member or friend.

There may be a number of home-based bakers in your community, and many of these bakers may be preparing the same products, but most likely each will have developed their own way to prepare the product that makes them stand out in the crowd. I am going to share one of my signature recipes with you. It is chocolate chip butter cookies, and it was once sold at a bakery in Southfield, Michigan. Over the years I have researched and played with a number of recipes until coming up with this one. The cookie is expensive to produce because it uses cake flour, and I no longer make it, but for rare occasions, I will pull it out since there is nothing on the market like it.

Chocolate Chip Butter Cookies
Yield: about 24 cookies

Ingredients
1 cup butter, softened
$2/3$ cup sugar
2 egg yolks
1 teaspoon almond extract
$2\frac{1}{2}$ cups sifted cake flour
$\frac{1}{4}$ teaspoon salt
$1\frac{1}{4}$ cups miniature chocolate morsels

Directions
1. Cream butter and sugar until fluffy (about 12 to 15 minutes)
2. Add egg yolks and extract. Beat well.

3. Stir flour and salt together.
4. Add flour mixture to egg and sugar mixture. The dough will be soft.
5. Wrap dough in plastic wrap and refrigerate for 1 hour.
6. Remove dough from the refrigerator. Roll it out to ½ inch thick.
7. Cut dough with 3-inch round cookie/biscuit cutters.
8. Place on ungreased nonstick cookie sheet.
9. Bake in a preheated 375-degree oven for 8 to 10 minutes or until delicately browned on edges.
10. Cool 15 to 20 minutes. Store in airtight container.

When developing your product line think in terms of categories. For example, learn to think in basic baking categories such as cakes, pies, cookies, bread, pastry, and candy; or concentrate on one or two baked goods and create separate product lines within those categories. If you are baking cakes, you may want to have two product lines. One may be pound cakes and the other may be frosted or iced cakes.

Pound Cakes
Brown Sugar Pound Cake
Five-Flavor Pound Cake
Fresh Apple Pound Cake

Frosted Cakes
Caramel Pecan Cake with Caramelized Icing
Carrot Cake with Butter Cream Frosting
Apple Cinnamon Spice Cake with Cream Cheese Frosting

When you first begin your home-based baking business, listen to your customers. Often the best and most profitable product ideas will come from your own customers. I love to bake all types of pies, but during the holidays I quickly learned that customers want familiar and traditional baked goods. They are willing to try the unusual items for themselves at various times of the year, but when it comes to serving family and friends, they want pumpkin, sweet potato, and pecan pies, especially in the fall. I rarely got a call for Double-Dutch Chocolate or an Old Southern Magnolia pie studded with walnuts. It helps to remember that, although you have multiple recipes in your repertoire, customers want what they like most, not necessarily what you like to bake most.

Pay attention to food trends and know what the most popular baked goods are for every season. If your baked goods are not in tune with the times, they may not sell. If you have a list of baked goods and no one is buying or inquiring, it's time to get out of the kitchen and start snooping around. Go to local farmer's markets, gourmet shops, and bakeries. Did a new bakery just open in your community? Stroll on in and see what they have to offer (and don't forget to make a purchase). You might be surprised to find that their products are as tasty as or better than your own. Perhaps the new baker at the farmer's market has put a twist on the cupcakes she sells or is providing gluten-free products. You will also want to subscribe to baking newsletters and magazines for professional bakers. These magazines generally report on baking trends and offer a good idea of what will be hot in the coming year.

Know your profit potential. Every home-based baker must determine the profit potential of each baked good. List all ingredients, packaging costs, printing, and shipping costs (if it's an item you plan to sell online). Consider how much of your (or someone else's) labor will be involved. Set a retail price appealing to customers and profitable to you, then double it to see if you'll be able to wholesale it. Then consider the market for your baked goods so you make sure you can produce the volume necessary to satisfy it. In other words, don't bite off more than you can chew. If you cannot bake more than four hours per day producing three large pound cakes, don't say you can do more, unless you have the baking capacity to do so. It is imperative to set realistic baking expectations.

Always locate more than one supplier for any ingredient or raw material used in your products and packaging. There is nothing worse than needing one hundred pie boxes only to learn that your local vendor is out of stock and you will need to purchase online and pay shipping and other fees. If you do not have a tax identification number for your business that qualifies you to purchase products wholesale, stock up on supplies when they go on sale and look for ways to lower the costs of your baked goods by comparison shopping.

Name your products appropriately. A name gives your baked goods personality, which in turn increases their salability. In developing new products, use humor whenever possible or appropriate. Do not overexaggerate the name of your product. Do not name a product after an ingredient if that specific ingredient is not in the product or its presence is sparse. Double Dutch Chocolate Blondie Bars is a great name if the bar is heavily laced with a stream of Dutch Chocolate like Droste Dutch unsweetened processed cocoa powder. If you only use a minute amount of cocoa powder in the product, this would not be the best name for the product, as customers' expectations may not be met.

One of the major legal issues that arises in home-based baking is selling cakes made with novelty-themed pans that have copyrighted art work stamped upon them. Unfortunately under no circumstances is anyone allowed to bake products and sell them for profit using cake pans that reflect copyrighted artwork. The licensor of that cake pan has copyrighted artwork, and their intended use is most likely for individual use in the home. It is illegal to reproduce the artwork for commercial sale without their written permission, and you will need to pay the licensor a portion of your profits if indeed they agree to negotiate a contract with your home-based bakery business.

A Word about Recipe Copyrights

Home-based bakers are often secretive of their signature recipes, and in my baking classes, one common question is "Can you really copyright a recipe?" Well, the answer is yes and no. You cannot copyright the listing of ingredients; however the directions and the actual procedure for putting the recipe together may be copyrighted.

According to Barbara Gibbs Ostmann and Jane L. Baker in *The Recipe Writers Handbook*, "The rule of thumb is that three major changes are required to make a recipe 'yours'." They also suggest that "even though you may make these changes as a professional courtesy, you should acknowledge the source or inspiration for the recipe."

If you are interested in learning more about what the United States Copyright Office says about recipe copyrights visit www.copyright.gov/fls/fl122.html.

Ask for Help and Get It

In all likelihood, you are a new home-based baker and starting a business for the first time. One of the most challenging obstacles to get past is the fear of failing and the fear associated with asking for help. Don't ever think you have to have all the answers; no one does. Don't think everything you do will work; it won't. Starting a home-based bakery business is no different from starting any small business. There will be ups and downs, disappointments and triumphs. Small business start-ups are challenging and fun, and they involve patience and perseverance. That is why, when you hit a bump in the road, it is imperative that you seek help. Learning how to ask for help and committing to learning how to do things right are critical to setting yourself up for success.

Never be afraid of seeming to be dumb or appearing to be unprofessional. Everyone started somewhere, and if you are going to operate a successful home-based bakery, you must get the help you need. One of the primary reasons good ideas don't get off the ground is fear, and you know what fear is? It's false evidence appearing real. Did you know we can—and do—talk ourselves out of great opportunities? How often have you thought about selling your delicious coconut cake, only to talk yourself out of it because you focus on all that can go wrong as opposed to assessing how you can jump over those hurdles and make the creative venture happen successfully?

The problem with fear is it will stop you dead in your tracks and kill your dreams. My question as you plan your home-based bakery is: "What's the basis for your fear?" Perhaps you need to really evaluate your plan and see where the fear is originating from. Are you not confident in your product or yourself? Do you lack family support for your venture?

Facing your fear and asking for help can show how smart you are and demonstrate that you've got good judgment and you're willing to admit that you know what you know and what you don't know. Plus, getting help up front will save you endless time, energy, and resources down the road.

When you need help, start your questions with what you do know and make sure you do your homework. Provide enough background information so you can put concern in the proper context. Give the person you are speaking to as much information as possible so they have a clear understanding of what it is that's missing and what exactly you need. Tell them what direction you want to take and ask for feedback or clarification. Don't just ask "How do I do this?" All too often, new start-ups don't get the information they need because they ask questions in such a manner that implies they want the solution to be handed over on a silver platter, and that will not happen.

If you don't know what direction to take, ask for tangible guidance. Instead of asking, "What should I do?" ask specifically, "What tools will I need to make the best decision?" or ask, "Where can I go to obtain the information I need?"

09

Selling Your Products Online

Online selling is no easy task. There are many advertisements out there that will tell you that you can make millions selling products online with little or no effort. Don't believe them. There is a lot of time, work, and effort that goes into online marketing and locating customers who are willing to part with their cold hard cash to purchase your baked goods online. You may not be able to sell millions, but selling thousands (perhaps even tens of thousands) might be an attainable goal.

In this chapter I will provide a brief overview of what you need to know regarding selling food products online, designing an e-commerce Web site, and policies you will need to have on your Web site to not only protect you and your customers but to ensure a sense of integrity. There are a number of ways to take your products to market, including food malls, malls selling handmade food products, direct sales, and affiliate programs.

The role of the Internet is driving every aspect of our economy. The rules guiding how we market, advertise, and sell are changing at warp speed. Today, the Internet is seen as a complement to virtually all business plans, influencing sales across other channels. According to Jupiter Media data that was presented at "The Secrets of Successful E-Retailers," a 2005 Winter Fancy Food Show Educational Program, for every dollar spent by consumers online, they spend an additional six dollars offline as a result of their online search. The issue is that "consumers want to determine how they'll do business with you—in your store, at a farmer's market location, or online, and an Internet purchase often increases the overall sales a person will do with you."

Consumers are becoming increasingly aware of online purchasing, and they now have much greater access to products that are unique, organic, and often customized to fit their individual needs. Huge companies that produce multiple products are finding themselves in competition with small mom-and-pop operations that specialize in offering superior services and products, usually for more money. You initially might think that would not be profitable for small businesses; however, for those discriminating consumers who seek quality over quantity, price point is not really an issue.

There is something to be said about purchasing a product sight unseen, and as a home-based baker there will be times when you will be selling to customers who have not tasted and/or seen your products . Take time to photograph your baked goods whenever possible so you can showcase them either online or in a portfolio. We all remember the days of mail-order, when a photograph in a catalog was the only way for a customer to see a product. In this industry a photograph really is worth a thousand words since customers may decide to order your decorated cookies, cakes, or cupcakes based on the photos of products made for other customers.

When taking photographs you do not need to use an expensive camera (a basic digital works well). Just try to get a close-up, crystal-clear photo of the product. I knew one home-based baker who asked a photography student at a local community college to photograph her wedding cakes in exchange for two dozen cupcakes. It was a win-win proposition.

Selling via Online Food Malls

Online food marketplaces (malls) like GourmetFoodMall.com and Foodzie.com provide a great way for small food producers to introduce their products to the general public. A major issue, however, is getting visitors to your particular location on the food mall Web site.

What's the traditional online business landscape like with a food mall? For a flat rate and/or a percentage of your profits you get:

- a Web page on the mall Web site
- a shopping cart/e-commerce system

You will need to market your products and services yourself, and one affordable method for getting the word out involves free online classifieds using sites like www.ebayclassifieds.com or www.oodle.com. Starting your own social network site is also an effective way to promote your products and get the word out about your baked goods. Social networking sites are usually free and simple to create. Some of the more popular sites are www.ning.com, www.facebook.com, and www.twitter

.com, a microblog that offers you an opportunity to share your day-to-day baking experiences with customers and potential customers.

The food malls/markets themselves attract shoppers, just like the traditional shopping malls of today, although they specifically focus on attracting foodies and those looking for unique food products that are not carried in traditional retail food outlets. The tenants of the food malls market themselves and attract business to their individual stores while simultaneously attracting shoppers to other businesses in the mall. A baker of scones, for instance, would probably get the attention of customers trolling the site for unique jellies, jams, and preserves.

One major issue with online food malls is that they can only feature so many products, so contact the mall owners to see what type of products they are interested in carrying. Some food malls have fees, others have no fees; you create your own profile and marketplace Web page on the site. Some may have listing fees for businesses who want to actually sell product through the Web site—an option worth considering for vendors who do not have their own individual Web site; selling through a food mall may be a great way to kick off an online presence.

An online presence is helpful for all home bakers, so whether you invest time and money in building a great standalone Web site or work with a food mall, the more exposure online the better; just make sure you are leveraging social media sites such as Ning, Facebook, and Twitter (see Chapter 6 for more information).

We mentioned earlier that PayPal provides an easy way for companies to start selling online, and if the food mall site you select has low or no fees, it may cost you next to nothing to join.

Here is a list of popular online malls that also sell food products:

- Etsy.com
- Foodzie.com
- GourmetFoodMall.com
- CarolinaFlavorsOnline.com
- TalkMarket.com

Developing a Web Site

If you do not have a Web site, you may want to either create a site yourself or hire a webmaster to create a Web site for you. Whichever option you choose, a substantial investment in time and money may be required for start-up costs, including:

- Domain name registration—A unique, case-insensitive name, consisting of a string made up of alphanumeric characters and dashes separated by periods, which the Domain Name System maps to IP numbers and other information; an identifier of a computer or site on the Internet.
- Site hosting—Once your Web site is completed, the site must be placed on a web server (a computer that is permanently connected to the Internet).
- E-commerce software—Software that will assist you in selling products online.
- Site development and maintenance—Upkeep of your Web site. The maintenance will involve making changes, editing, and adding widgets and other systems to enhance your site usability.
- Marketing—The commercial processes involved in promoting, selling, and distributing your product or service.
- Credit card transaction fees—Fees paid to accept credit card transactions; paid to the bank or other outside vendor.
- Internet access—Being able to log on to the Internet.

How to Obtain a Domain Name

- Go to the Web site of an authorized registrar, such as www.godaddy.com, www.register.com, or www.whois.net. You can also Google "domain names" to find a registrar or ask someone who has a domain name to recommend a site.

- Use the registrar's online search function to see if your desired domain name is taken.

- If your domain name is available, follow the registrar's instructions to complete the registration form and pay by credit card.

You obtain a domain name for a period of one to ten years. If a domain name owner (the "registrant") fails to renew the domain name at the end of its term, the registration of the domain name will be revoked and the domain name may be acquired by another party.

Web Site Checklist

Use this checklist when developing your new Web site. There are several things that you need to think about; this list will help you stay focused and organized.

	Task	☑
1.	Determine the purpose of your Web site (Is it strictly for information or is it an e-commerce site that will allow you to sell your product online?)	☐
2.	Determine your target market and their specific needs (Will your customers want/be willing to purchase in advance and pay online via your Web site?)	☐
3.	Come up with several goals (short-term and long-term) for your Web site (Will a one-page introduction suffice or do you need multiple Web pages?)	☐
4.	Research hosting companies based on your specific needs.	☐
5.	Research e-commerce solutions based on your specific needs, for example, www.paypal.com; VeriSign, www.verisign.com; and Authorize.net, www.authorize.net/. (E-commerce solutions are companies that provide ways for small business owners to accept credit card and electronic payments for goods and services, along with mobile payments.)	☐
6.	Research a web developer based on your specific needs. (Is building your own Web site something you can do yourself?)	☐
7.	Develop the architecture of your Web site. (How will your pages flow from one to the other?)	☐
8.	Create content for each of your pages and ensure that it is proofread and spell-checked. (Can you write this information or will you need to ask someone else to help you?)	☐
9.	Decide if you need any type of programming, and if so, research programmers that can provide a product that fits your specific needs.	☐

10.	Create the artwork and graphics that will be used on your Web site. You may need to take photographs of your products; however do NOT use images from other Web sites without the owner's permission.	☐
11.	Research domain names for your Web site; will you use .com, .net, .org? Dot-com is usually used for commercial businesses, which includes home-based bakeries. Dot-net is used for commercial businesses when the dot-com is not available, and dot-org is used for not-for-profit organizations.	☐

(Table provided with permission from Stiletto Media Group © 2008)

The time spent on design, taking photos of products, and updating the site should also be taken into consideration. If you want to design a sleek, professional, easy-to-navigate site that loads quickly at both dial-up and broadband speeds, you will probably need a webmaster (unless you have considerable computer design skills).

You will need to register your URL on all the major search engines (including Google.com and Yahoo.com) to make sure your site shows up in relevant searches. If you are not computer savvy, you will want to browse the Internet and read up on how to register your URL on search engines and learn about the importance of keywords that should be used on your Web site. There is a free online course that provides information on the ABCs of Web design that may be helpful as you build your online presence; visit www.w3schools.com/ for more information. Even if you hire a professional Web site developer, there are a number of things you should make sure to include in your new Web site.

You might want to take the time to gather information about designing your Web site yourself. You can try using the Web site development programs offered by www.google.com and http://wordpress.org.

As you think about designing your Web site, consider the following:

- Domain name.
- Hosting site (shop around for the best price).

- E-commerce software—e.g., PayPal (investigate how customers will pay for your products).
- Who will be your webmaster? (Locate a webmaster if you need one.)
- Determine a payment method: It could be PayPal, or you may also want to speak with your banker about the best payment method for your business. Remember to also ask about all fees, upfront and hidden.

Establishing a Web Site Presence

As you establish your Web site, it is imperative that you create compelling copy to post on your site. It is not enough to just welcome visitors and say "Okay, now buy my cupcakes, cookies, and muffins." Do you know how people are using your product? Or what they are looking for in a product? Pay close attention to the words you use to describe your baked goods; also take note of what words your competitors use to describe their offerings. Compelling offers and ideal keywords spark attention.

Entice your Web site visitors to action and give them what they want the way they want it. You may have the best pound cake in the world, but if it is not the flavor, texture, and size the consumer wants, it will not sell well. Brand your name, product, and superior quality into the minds of your customers. Branding is what sets you apart from your competition. It is building a familiarity and comfort with your company and products. The idea is for your customers to see your "brand"— your company name, logo, or product—and associate it with something that signifies all that is good. You want to create an emotional connection and a unique experience for your customer.

It's also important to establish trust and give your customers a sense of security. Post your privacy policy prominently and have customer service information clearly displayed, along with shipping information, so customers know you will provide a quick response. Set up a secure server to handle credit card transactions. Make every effort to answer customer queries by phone or e-mail promptly, effectively, and courteously.

Providing a Safe Shopping Experience

You will always have customers who do not feel online shopping is safe and who voice their concerns about identity theft and fraud. To assuage such fears, you should provide the option of making a purchase over the phone by posting a visible contact number throughout the site and checkout process. Allow customers to fill in their order online, minus credit card details, and then request a call back from you. Making your site as trustworthy and transparent as possible, and addressing concerns about fraud and security, may persuade some otherwise cautious shoppers to go ahead and make a purchase. Provide reassurance throughout the site, especially on product and payment pages about privacy and security issues. Add third-party verification logos such as VeriSign (a technology company that specializes in data encryption and e-commerce), which provide evidence that a site can be trusted. Shoppers also want to see contact details for reassurance that they can get in touch with a person if something goes wrong with an order.

Some shoppers who are reluctant to enter credit or debit card details may be persuaded to buy if your site offers a payment method such as PayPal or Google Checkout. This may also increase conversions; in a recent national survey by TrialPay, 59 percent of respondents said they would be more likely to buy online if alternative methods like Google Checkout and PayPal were available.

How to Set Up PayPal

You will need:
A bank account
Your bank routing number
Your bank account number
Your contact information

Please read through the PayPal information (www.paypal.com) carefully. Setting up your PayPal account is not difficult and can be done completely online. The secure online portal provides a demonstration that walks you though creating your account, making it easy for customers to pay for your products and services.

Another way to make online customers more comfortable with purchasing your baked goods online is to choose shopping cart software that allows them to navigate through your product selection quickly and easily. However, keep in mind that there's nothing worse than purchasing shopping cart software, then finding yourself unable to reach the developers or technical support team when you have a problem.

You must determine what you are willing to spend for the various options and functionalities. Shopping cart software costs range from free to tens of thousands of dollars. Developing a custom cart from the ground up can cost even more. The free options may sound good at first until you run into problems or need support that is nonexistent, so buyer beware!

Technical support for a cart is probably the most important aspect of your e-commerce site development. If you have a problem (and you will), does the software provider provide live support? Do they have a phone number on the Web site to address technical support issues? Is there a fee for technical support access?

You may be surprised by the number of software providers that do not even provide a phone number and rarely respond to e-mail inquiries, so shop around carefully before you consider making a purchase. The shopping cart should be professionally installed on your server by a qualified server administrator or the cart software programmer. There are typically many server/cart configuration options that can be very confusing if you are not familiar with the environment.

A database will also need to be set up and tied into your cart. Also be sure to choose a cart that is compatible with your server operating system. Typically, Linux servers will run PHP and Perl solutions, and Windows servers will use .ASP and .NET applications.

Shipping Your Online Orders

Choose a vendor to ship your product. Keep in mind the shelf life of your product and know that your baked goods must not only be shipped quickly but safely. No one wants to receive a pound cake that is broken into pieces. Here are some basic shipping services to consider:

UPS: www.ups.com/

Federal Express: http://fedex.com/us/

United States Postal Service (USPS): www.usps.com/

DHL: www.dhl.com/en.html

Some of the shipping options include: ground, first class, home delivery, express, priority, two-day, and overnight delivery, depending on the shipping vendor you select.

- Live rate lookup—means that it will return a shipping cost to the customer based on the actual product weight plus packaging.
- Weight-based table—means if a product weighs 3 pounds, the shipping price is $9.50 or some other set price.
- Price-based table—means if the price of the baked good is $29.95 or less it will ship for $9.50 or some other set price.

A Word about Shipping

Examine your product carefully. Selling your product directly to a local consumer is much easier than packaging your product for a cross-country journey. If you want to make sure your baked goods don't end up as crumbs by the time they get to their destination, think about the type of product you plan to ship and how it must be wrapped and packaged.

Here are a few guidelines to follow when shipping baked goods:

- Sturdiness is key. (The more sturdy the actual product the better it will ship.)
- Unless you are freezing your product solid, avoid using decorations, icings, etc.
- Frosted cookies ship fine as long as you use royal icing, a decorating icing made from powdered sugar, meringue powder, and lemon juice.
- Secure a tight fit. (Whether shipped by the U.S. Postal Service or a private carrier, your package will travel along sundry conveyor belts, be exposed to hot and/or cold, get handled by several people, and possibly rattle for many miles in the back of a truck.)
- Small, thick cookies are less likely to break than large, thinner cookies.
- Don't mix soft and hard cookies in the same container; the moisture in the soft cookies can make hard cookies, such as biscotti, become soft.

The UPS Store has compiled a list of cookies its shippers say can take the tumbling and temperatures. They recommend molasses cookies, peanut butter cookies, shortbread, sugar cookies, brownies, biscotti, and puffed rice treats. I do not know how accurate this listing is, however, so test-ship your product first (preferably under various weather conditions over varying distances) before even considering online sales.

I have learned from experience that the best baked goods for shipping are drop cookies, bar cookies, pound cakes, and Bundt cakes, all of which tend to be thick and dense.

If you are not placing products in a can or other protective container, the key is it to wrap each baked item individually in FDA-approved wrapping. Cookies as well as cakes can be cushioned using bubble wrap or foam peanuts. Remember, bubble wrap and peanuts cannot touch the actual food product, since they are not FDA-approved. If you are interested in how food products sold online are packaged and shipped, one good way to find out is to order a product or two from a competitor.

Remember that all of the variables just discussed will impact your shipping costs along with package size and any handling charges you may add on because special handling is needed to carefully wrap products. Nothing, however, beats a trial shipment or two before you officially offer online sales and shipping of your products.

Food Photography: Images on the Web

When selling your products via your Web site, you will need product images. A professional photographer is recommended. It is essential that your photos be of top quality. A poor quality image looks unprofessional and will not help sell your baked goods. However, if you choose to take the photos yourself, try and follow these guidelines. (If you are not much of a shutterbug, you can consider taking a photography class at your local community center.)

- Use light backdrops (not white).
- Try to use natural sunlight or studio lights that produce no shadows.
- You will need a thumbnail image and a larger detailed image. There is a variety of good photo-editing software on the market. Paint Shop Pro is a good, low-cost, multipurpose photo editing tool.
- Adobe Photoshop is the top-of-the-line software tool for photo editing, retouching, and compressing your images.

Once you decide to place images of your baked goods on your Web site, know that each product will need a brief written description. You want to attract and intrigue potential customers, so be sure to use interesting copy that is full of adjectives and possibly a bulleted list of features as part of the description:

Lemon and Lavender Pound Cake—Our signature Lemon and Lavender Pound Cake blends the subtle flavors of lemon with a hint of dried lavender making this the perfect ending to any meal.

* * Moist and sweet*

* * Light lemon glaze*

* * Serving Options: This pound cake is delicious toasted and served with whipped butter.*

Learning from Your Online Competitors

A home-based baker usually does not have the budget to hire marketing professionals who can research the competition and seek out what they are preparing and what specialized ingredients they are using. So you're probably on your own to check out and size up your competition. The knowledge you gain about competing home-based bakers/bakeries is extremely important, especially since it will help you carve your own product niche in the marketplace.

Think for a moment: If you want to get someone a box of custom decorated cookies, where would you go? Ask yourself, "What do I want my customers to come to me for?" Once upon a time in my community I was known as the "pie lady." Is there something that you will specialize in and be known for? One of the best ways to monitor what food processors are doing and selling is to visit a number of the food malls where many small food processors sell their products. You will then be able to view what is being sold and how products are packaged. It may prove beneficial to order from the competitor to see how the product ships and how the competitors' product tastes. Visit www.gourmetfoodmall.com, www.foodzie.com, or www.fooducopia.com.

Monitor the way your competitors do business, and pay close attention to these six factors, which can assist you in planning your home-based bakery business:

1. Who is your competition?

Do you know who owns the competing home-based bakery in your community? How many home-based bakers are in direct competition with you? Do you sell similar or the same types of products? One of the best ways to learn this information is from their Web sites, their social networking sites, or by visiting their tables if they sell at the farmer's market. You may discover that the baker only works on the weekends, or perhaps baking is just a hobby for the summer. Knowing why a home-based baker bakes will help you plan how you will develop your own bakery business in the same market. A home-based baker enrolled in my online class was a professional baker and wanted to bake from home until she could locate a brick-and-mortar location. Her goal was to open a small pastry shop and sell wholesale. She had no intention of being open to the public, but she wanted to deliver baked goods to coffee shops, small restaurants, and hotels in her downtown area. She did not care about competing with other home-based bakers, since her goals were completely different from the home bakers in her community.

Another way to learn about your competition is to Google them. If your competition has been written up in the local newspaper or appeared on the television or radio, there may be some write-up or mention online referring to it. The more you know about the competition, the better. Today everyone is competing for a limited number of resources. There are only so many birthday cakes, pies, custom decorated cookies, and pastries the consumer will purchase on any given day. As a home-based baker, you compete for sales, customers' time, and the opportunity to brand your little bakery as a "pillar" in the community; and your competition is anyone who prevents you from getting that recognition.

2. Pay attention

Pay close attention to the products and services your competitor provides and how they market them to customers. For example, if you visit your local farmer's market, and one of your competitors is selling product hand over fist, you should stroll over and see what is happening. Sometimes it might be nothing more than new packaging or a lovely array of sampling trays. While you are standing there with no samples, she might be giving away a free cookie with every product sold. Everyone wants something for nothing, or at least the appearance that they are getting something for nothing. I know one home-based baker who piped tiny carrots on the top of her carrot cake while her competitor did not. The tiny carrots not only made a statement, they were cute and appealing.

3. The price must be right

The price you charge for your products will have a profound impact on whether or not your products sell. If you price your baked goods too high, no one will purchase them; and if you price them too low, customers will think they lack quality. Pricing will be one of the most challenging parts of setting up your home-based bakery business. There is no real right or wrong strategy. We talked earlier about covering all your costs and setting a price that allows you to make money; anything less is pointless. With that said, there are always exceptions to the pricing rule, and it often depends on where you are selling your products.

If you are selling at a farmer's market, you can leave yourself room to carefully negotiate a lower price if it is in your best interest to do so. The operative principle here is called "saving face." In other words, you will only lower your price if you can save face, i.e., maintain the integrity of your basic pricing structure. So you tell your customer, "I only accept a lower price under the following circumstances . . ." What are those circumstances? You might consider offering a discount if the customer will buy more than one, or if the merchandise is flawed (broken cookies) or if it is the end of the day and you do not want to take products home with you. Remember, your products are highly perishable and will not last long anyway. The key here is to bring to the farmer's market what you think you can sell. If you run out of baked goods, you can always provide customers with a business card or refer them to your Web site and ask them to order online and schedule a pick-up the next time they are at the farmer's market.

Never try to undercut your competition for the sake of getting a sale. If you sell jumbo chocolate chip cookies for $1.95 per cookie and your competitor is selling chocolate chip cookies that are smaller at two for $1.95, stand your ground and see what your customers want. Sometimes the old adage "more is better" works, but sometimes it really depends on the quality of the product.

4. Dress for success

How your competitor packages products and delivers them is also something you need to pay close attention to, since you want to design your packaging as well or better. The packaging does not have to be expensive or fancy, but it should be neat and appealing. There are some home-based bakers who do not deliver and only sell from a designated location like a farm stand, farmer's market, or through a local cafe or coffee shop. Other home-based bakers deliver all of their baked goods because they want to get to know their customers and develop good relationships with them. This builds a strong customer bond and also helps develop a brand.

Selling Online

Every e-commerce site should have the following:

Privacy Policy
A privacy policy is a legal document that details information related to customers' and merchants' private profiles.

Shipping Terms and Conditions
These are the rules and regulations you create regarding how you will ship your product, including but not limited to packaging requirements, shipment delivery, and damaged products.

Payment Options
Your payment options policy tells customers how they can pay for your products, e.g., PayPal, MasterCard, Visa, electronic check, etc.

Contact Information
Contact information should be listed on every piece of correspondence and on your Web site. Customers should always know how to contact your company.

FAQs
Every business that does business online and many that don't should have an FAQ section to address common questions.

Customer Service Page
Either as a page on its own or as part of the FAQs, you should list your policy regarding customer service issues.

5. Develop a competitive edge
Have you looked into the devices your competitor uses to enhance customer loyalty and the additional services they offer their customers? I know a home-based baker

who will score her cakes so it is easier for her customers to serve professional looking slices. There is another home-based baker who offers a dessert-of-the-month program so her products are in the homes of her customers every month. This may not appear to be much, but it is the little things that really do take you over the top when it comes to satisfying your customer. Think about what a business owner has done for you that either made you feel like an appreciated customer or provided you with service above and beyond what is typically necessary. Are you willing to do that for your customers? If the answer is yes, then you are on your way to gaining a competitive edge.

Does your competitor use innovative business practices? Some home-based bakers attempt to make every effort to accommodate their customers when it comes to paying for products. Do you know if your competition takes checks and/or credit cards? Is your home-based bakery business going to be cash-and-carry only? Offering multiple ways to pay for your baked goods will allow customers to order more often and place orders for special occasions. There is always a slight credit risk, but if you're careful, expanding the number of ways customers can pay almost always works to your advantage.

I learned quickly that at my local farmer's market many customers did not want to pay cash, they wanted to write a check or pay using a credit card; plus there are times when customers run out of cash and don't want to use an ATM but instead pay with credit. As a business owner it is in your best interests to accommodate customers to the best of your ability.

6. Use social networking to drum up business

Does your competitor use social networking groups to drum up new customers? Many home-based bakers think it is essential to have a Web site, but until you can afford one, you might want to join or start a social networking group or fan club.

Social networking has evolved and grown rapidly in recent years, providing huge potential for businesses to cheaply and effectively market online. Those that have used social marketing often improve their business performance. It's one of the fastest modes of word-of-mouth advertising. If one of your customers gives you a good review, the second person in turn may stop by to visit your Web site or Facebook page. Social networking sites are great places to find potential customers, and finding qualified customers to purchase your baked goods is half the battle.

One home-based baker who uses social networking successfully is Andrea Bigelow of Durham, North Carolina. Andrea keeps family, friends, and customers up-to-date with her home-based baking products and announces any new additions to her bakery menu using Facebook. The Twisted Sisters Barkery, owned by Teresa Hunt, Pam Ray, and Diane Willis, uses Facebook not only to spread the word about their delicious dog treats, but to post photos of their day at the local farmer's market or community event. If your competitor has a Web site, MySpace, or Facebook page, see if you can locate it and view the information and conversations they have with the people who are following them. Are they on Twitter? Do they send out a monthly online newsletter? Knowing what the competition is doing will certainly help you devise a more effective way to get the word out about your products.

Everything that is said about you and your competitor is meaningful, since a negative comment can provide you with an opportunity to improve upon your competitors' practices and a compliment can provide you with strategies that their customers enjoy. I know one home-based baker who sends out a newsletter about her baked goods well in advance of major holidays. She does this to pique interest, and she builds a buzz around her upcoming new products. When it comes time for customers to order their products, she is usually busy long before her competitors. She has laid the foundation and keeps her bakery on the minds and taste buds of her customers.

10 Interviews with Home-Based Bakers

One of the best ways to learn about home-based baking is reading interviews like the ones below from other bakers, learning what worked and what did not work and the resources they used to make their baking business a success. Some bakers bake as a hobby, while others operate full-fledged bakery businesses. Over the course of several years, I have interviewed home-based bakers to learn how they got started and what motivates them to grow their home-based baking businesses. Here are the stories of four home-based bakers and one kitchen incubator owner, and how they went from kitchen to market.

Lilian Chavira, Owner, Gellocake

How did you learn to decorate cakes? Did you take a class?

I do believe that I got this artistic gift from my parents, who happen to be excellent cooks. I learned to make desserts as a little girl. At that time, it was like a game to me! I was extremely shy, and making these sweets helped me to express myself to friends and loved ones. My mom's kitchen was the haven where I spent time experimenting, especially with Jell-O gelatin. I started decorating gelatins for family reunions, using all kinds of fruits, making different shapes, trying different color combinations, and experimenting with unique flavors. Little by little, with practice I improved.

I did not start decorating cakes with frosting until three years ago. I decided to start baking the cakes for my own kids' birthday parties. Just for fun! I took two levels of the Wilton course, which gave me the basics. I realized then that this was something I really *loved* to do.

Now, Gellocake is giving me the opportunity to keep improving my skills as the business grows and as new challenges present themselves daily.

What type of icing do you use? Your baked goods look picture perfect.

When I started with the cake-decorating classes, I found that some of the icings are made with shortening. Although it gives a better consistency, I have always felt that desserts do not have to be so *greasy*. I decided instead to use butter or cream cheese. The cream cheese is actually a favorite request by my customers.

How did you come up with the idea for Gellocake?

In 2004, the company that my husband worked for transferred him from Mexico/El Paso, Texas to Okemos, Michigan. I then resigned my job as a graphic designer in the marketing department of an American-Swedish company. As a stay-at-home mom, I felt the need to remain creative. At the same time I had the desire to keep alive the memories of the wonderful creative times I had growing up with my parents. So, I returned to my kitchen haven!

Designing desserts allowed me to express myself again. I made gelatins and cakes for playgroups, church potlucks, and as gifts for teachers and neighbors. I enjoyed every opportunity that I had to bake and design for those who were so special to me.

Suddenly, I was surrounded by treasured friends who encouraged me to sell my creations. They pushed me, my husband supported me, and my kids inspired me! One day, the dream to have a home-based bakery became my prayer. I decided to put it in God's hands and was prepared to do whatever it would take to make it happen.

I came up with the business name, *Gellocake,* by combining my two different signature desserts—*gelatins* and *cakes*. With the name in place, I became inspired to jump over every hurdle that presented itself along the way. After that, it took me almost eight months of planning and getting all the permits from the different governmental entities to build my new, separate industrial kitchen. It was not an easy process, but I am so thankful to the state of Michigan for making it possible! My reward was seeing "Gellocake—Gourmet Gelatins & Cakes" become a reality.

Where do you get your ideas and inspiration for your baked goods?

Everywhere! As I mentioned, most of my gelatins are my own experiments. I also have other traditional desserts like my Flan, which is a traditional Mexican sweet, or my Cream Cheese Pound Cake with Raspberries, which has become a favorite of Michigan's berry lovers. I just keep my eyes and ears really open to see and listen to what my friends and customers want. When I bake for kids, I think about my own little ones and ask myself what would make them happy. When I receive a call for a custom cake, dessert table, or corporate event, I take time to make sure that my design will be more than just a traditional cake. I want to make every customer feel unique and extremely special. It is always a joy to see them surprised and thrilled at their celebration. My goal is to make every dessert an expression of art and passion!

Do you allow your customers to come to your home? Why or why not?

Yes, most of my customers actually come to my house to pick their orders up. I just encourage appointments. For the catering service part of the business, I make trips to the venues to design the dessert tables. In those cases, I deliver and set up all the requested desserts and decorations. It is important to be in communication with the customer every step of the way and to visit the venue with them before the day of the event.

Did you always have a Web site?

No, when I started, all my funds were invested in the construction of my industrial kitchen. I did not have one more penny to spend. I got my Web page after six months in business with the help of a wonderful friend who was starting her own graphic design company.

Do you think a Web site is really needed? Why or why not?

I think it definitely helps. New customers will see your business as an established bakery. The Web site is also a great tool for communicating with the public. With pictures in place, customers can see what they would like to order. However, I would recommend that new bakers look for creative ways to build their Web site inexpensively. They could find a new entrepreneur who is starting his own business or a student who could keep it simple and not pricey. Remember, we need to take one step at a time!

How did you learn to price your goods? Do you use some type of formula to derive a price?

In my case, competitors are a key element to check out. I am one block away from one of the best bakeries in town. Their cakes are excellent and have similar quality and gourmet presentation as mine. That was an important factor to consider.

I also consulted with friends who have experience in the field. Chefs and caterers have a good perspective on the options in the market. We need to keep in mind that at the beginning we cannot expect to be making huge profit. We want people to first try out our product.

My best support on that matter (and others), however, came from my business consultant from the Michigan Small Business and Technology Development Center. I strongly recommend that new business owners contact these types of organizations; they can provide excellent and valuable advice on the entire process. Their help is not only free but it is professional and wonderful.

Do you bake on demand when you get an order, or just bake on certain days?
My desserts are custom-made. I do not store them in the freezer or refrigerator. I make them on demand so that they are always fresh.

Do you ship throughout the United States or locally? Where do you get your shipping supplies from?
I do not ship my products at all. My gourmet gelatins are fragile; they could be damaged easily. However, I always like to embark on new challenges. I will not reject the possibility of distributing Gellocakes throughout the country in the future.

How long have you been operating your home-based bakery?
Gellocake's inauguration was on June 14, 2008.

Do you make customers sign a contract?
I do not ask customers to sign contracts for regular orders, which usually are placed by phone or e-mail. I have requested signatures, though, with dessert tables or bigger cakes where 50 percent advance payment is required. However, I know that as the business gets bigger, this will become a requirement.

What is the most rewarding thing about operating a home-based bakery?
It is an excellent way to start! First of all, I control my own schedule. I am able to spend time with my young kids. I can still help them with homework, attend field trips, participate in school and after-school activities, and get involved in their daily routines. Second, the pressure and stress of rent and other high overhead expenses are eliminated. Third, I get the chance to learn gradually from my own experiences. I can see what works and what needs to be improved upon or changed.

What is the biggest obstacle?

My biggest obstacle so far has been advertising. In my case, I do not get clients who just happen to be passing by. I don't have a window display to attract love-at-first-sight customers. I fully depend on my customer recommendations. In addition, I am trying to be creative and develop my marketing skills for the business using inexpensive tools. The money and resources are still limited.

Another obstacle I face comes with the advance notice that I need to prepare my desserts. Due to their busy schedules, some customers fail to take time out to place their orders. They think about the dessert only at the last minute. Consequently, I lose their business to competitors that have commercial establishments. Although, starting small is an excellent way to start; I look forward to moving to a bigger, beautiful store-front bakery someday. That will come at the right time!

How do you market your business? To promote Gellocake, I have designed attractive business cards, brochures, and flyers, which I distribute to my current customers and hand out during events. I also e-mail monthly newsletters to stay in constant contact. I include information about upcoming events, pictures of new designs, and special promotions. I have contacted local newspapers and magazines that publish free press releases.

The most successful promotion tool for Gellocake so far has been word of mouth. I, however, realized that my customer/friend base was not enough. I still needed to spread the news out further. I checked out the information tools available in my area of need using every resource I could find that the government of Michigan offers. Some of them are: MI-SBTDC (Michigan Small Business Technology Development Center), Lansing Community College (Own your business, own your future), The Meridian Asset Resource Center (MARC) (a public/private partnership created to help entrepreneurial efforts within Meridian Township, www.themarc.biz/), and Okemos Public Library. I also joined a local business association, Zonta Club of Meridian East, which is an international organization of executives and professional women.

I have made wonderful contacts through these options in addition to having good friends who have stuck with me and understood how challenging starting a new business can be. They are helping to market my bakery! I have gotten some of my biggest events and most loyal customers through these resources. Every state in the country is creating ways to support new small business owners. But we need to take the initiative to find them. I have learned to be patient, creative, and to always remember that there is a time "to seed" and a time "to harvest"!

Diane Purkey, Owner, Maine's Cakes & Cookies

Diane Purkey, the owner and operator of Maine's Cakes & Cookies, has done a remarkable job building her home-based bakery business and providing quality products to her community and those outside her community. Diane ships her custom cookies all over the country and has learned by trial and error what works and what does not work as it relates to the unique work of baking for profit.

Diane is a small business owner who loves what she does and considers herself very lucky to be doing what she loves for a living. As you browse her vast collection of custom cookies, you can't help but be struck by the craftsmanship that goes into her products. Recently I e-mailed a number of questions to Diane from both my online and face-to-face classes, and she took time out of her busy schedule to share insight into the wonderful world of home-based baking.

What type of icing do you use? They look picture perfect.

Thank you! I use royal icing—confectioner's sugar, meringue powder, water, and gel food colors. A couple of suggestions: Keep your mixing bowl, beater, and decorating tips completely grease-free, and use filtered non-mineral water. This will keep your icing from drying with splotchy areas on them!

How did you learn about shipping your cookies?

Trial and error. You learn in a hurry what works and what definitely does not work! I shipped to myself, then to family and friends until I got it right.

What carrier do you use?

U.S. Postal Service Priority Mail.

Do your cookies ever break?

Very rarely—I take great care in packaging the cookies—first individual cellophane-bag wrapping, then each cookie is wrapped with bubble wrap. The box is lined with bubble wrap and then surrounded with Styrofoam peanuts. The packaging and packing materials are very expensive, but they get the job done. The packaging/packing costs are a large part in the pricing of the cookie.

Do you allow your customers to come to your home?

Yes. I live in rural Maine, so this does not happen very often, but two or three times a year a client will opt to pick up an order rather than have it shipped. My kitchen is licensed and inspected by the State of Maine, and Maine Cakes & Cookies carries the proper insurance coverage for this.

Did you always have a Web site?

Yes.

Do you think a Web site is really needed?

Yes!

Do you bake every day or certain days of the week?

I bake/decorate/package every day except Sunday, but when I'm super busy, even Sunday.

Do you bake on demand when you get an order?

I bake to order. Sometimes that is ASAP, but usually clients have reserved my time by deposit several weeks or months ahead, so I usually know what needs to be done each week. There are several times during the year when I am completely booked and have to turn client orders away.

Do you ship outside the United States?

Rarely, but yes. I use Federal Express for this, and the client is responsible for all customs fees and forms.

Where do you get your shipping supplies from?

The boxes are supplied by the U.S. Postal Service for Priority Mail shipping, so currently they are free of charge. All other boxes and bubble wrap I buy from ULine .com. Comparison shop your packaging supplies with shipping added. They are very expensive.

How long have you been operating a home-based bakery?

I obtained my license as a home processor from the State of Maine June 2, 2003, and started selling cookies and cakes later that summer.

What is the most rewarding thing about operating a home-based bakery?

Happy clients! When you get a note or phone call and the client says "WOW, the cookies are perfect, thank you so much for making my day so special," or when setting up a wedding cake, the bride runs towards you, jumping and smiling, saying, "It is perfect, exactly what I envisioned" and then gives you a big hug.

What is the biggest obstacle?

Storage. There is never enough storage.

Do you ship cakes?

I ship pound cakes in decorative boxes and tins.

Abraham Palmer, Owner, The Box Turtle Bakery

The following excerpt was provided by Mr. Palmer:

The vision for the bakery was built around three things: freshly milled whole grains, baking in a masonry oven, and local foods. The importance of whole grains is generally understood, but their typical preparation destroys much of the benefits. The masonry oven is very traditional for bread baking, and the design has stayed in use with good reason. Finally my focus on local starts at the beginning with locally grown grains and continues with as many other local ingredients as I can find.

The business was started gradually while I continued my full-time job over the course of more than a year. I had to select wheat varieties, find a farmer to grow them, obtain a seed cleaner, set up grain storage, obtain a mill, build a masonry oven, modify my home, obtain the necessary equipment, and perform the other standard business start-up items.

My target market can be summarized simply: local, local, and local. I target local families in my town of about twenty thousand. As of now, I have only been open three months, but my plans also include local farmer's markets and businesses that enthusiastically support the purchase of locally produced foods. Changing of individual buying habits and the recognition of nutritional benefits appears to be slow work.

Longer term, I still see myself operating as a home-based bakery. I will hopefully have inspired some others to try this same model and have been able to help them get off the ground with their own bakeries. I also see myself continuing to strengthen and diversify the grains grown locally. I hope that, by continuing to operate as a small bakery and being willing to modify recipes and techniques based on individual crops, I can provide a key bridge between heirloom grains in seed banks and new research trials, and the growing of these grains as a larger commodity. (Visit The Box Turtle Bakery at www.boxturtlebakery.com/.)

Teresa Hunt, Pam Ray, and Diane Willis, Owners, Twisted Sisters Barkery

This is the story of three home-based bakers who discovered they could not sell their baked goods because they had indoor pets. The three women decided to take their disappointment and turn it into a different kind of bakery.

For three longtime friends in the city of Raleigh, North Carolina—Pam Ray, Teresa Hunt, and Diane Willis—business has gone to the dogs, literally. These three women have launched a dog treat company affectionately call Twisted Sisters Barkery, offering even the most finicky Fidos a natural, uniquely flavored, preservative-free alternative to today's grocery store dog treats.

The three college friends refer to themselves as *twisted* because they have passed the true test of time, remaining friends for nearly thirty years through many of life's twists and turns. And they are *sisters* because, as you talk to these women, their bond is obvious. You quickly find yourself caught up in their infectious laughter and excitement. They chose the word *barkery*, because it's all about the dogs—their dogs to be exact: Pru, Pearl, Katie, and Purdie. It all adds up to a life's journey fulfilled.

The journey began decades ago, as they frequently talked of going into business together pursuing their passion to bake, but the timing and circumstances never felt right. As the years passed, this restless urge grew even stronger, and the Sisters began to plan their work and work their plan.

It began by enrolling in a class in Cary, North Carolina. Their instructor (who happens to be the author of this book) taught these aspiring food entrepreneurs what resources and materials they needed to help start and run a profitable food business from home. Months went into research and testing, samplings, and tastings, all the while keeping true to what they were looking for in healthy alternative treats for their own dogs. They worked on treats void of added sugars, salts, and preservatives. They also focused on treats that were freshly baked as opposed to ones with never-ending shelf lives; and treats with ingredients that you could easily identify and pronounce, such as sweet potato, rice, cinnamon, and honey.

Their home-baked treats can currently be found at the local farmer's market and at special events around the Raleigh area in what they call a "barker's dozen" of thirteen. Their baked goodies come in the K-9 signature flavors developed by the Sisters themselves, including Twenty-Furr K Goldfish with natural aged cheddar, the Banana Blue Moon Pie with banana and coconut, the Hawaiian Barkquet with passion fruit and honey, the Veggiemite Bite with rosemary and sage, the Fruitie Nilla Woofer with cranberry and orange, the Nacho Nibbler with cheddar and tomato, the Barkanator with chicken stock and carrot, the Howling Hound Bone with sweet potato and cinnamon, and the Nutter Bone with peanut butter, cinnamon, and honey.

Each treat is slowly baked, basted, and hand-cut. They are colored with natural food colorings, using nothing artificial and are just as aromatic and eye-catching as their names imply. They are freshly baked, natural, and preservative-free with flavor combinations that you will not typically find on your grocer's shelves, and they have proven to be a hit with the palates of canine clients.

You can visit the Twisted Sisters Barkery on Facebook, where they share their love for healthy dog treats with animal lovers nationwide.

Sandie Nathan, Owner, Elixir Kitchen Space

Recently, food entrepreneurs have been popping up everywhere; but unfortunately not everyone has the ability or resources to start a home-based bakery from their home kitchens. For some gifted bakers, the only way to prepare their culinary masterpieces and share them with the world is to find a kitchen incubator that will allow them to bake or cook for a marginal fee. The incubator business is rarely written about; in fact, you may not even know of its existence. I recently discovered an interesting Web site that features a kitchen incubator in Fort Worth, Texas. Sandie Nathan, owner and operator of Elixir Kitchen Space, took time out of her busy day to share what really goes on in kitchen incubators.

How did you start this wonderful business?

I have always loved to cook and bake, so after working in the information technology industry for about ten years, I decided to attend culinary school at night to see if it was something I could turn into a career that I would enjoy. My passion for baking really took off, so I started to form a plan to start baking part-time while still keeping my day job. I found out that in Texas, you are not allowed to sell food you make at home, so I began my search for somewhere to bake. I contacted restaurants—they let me bake in the wee hours of the morning when they were closed—and some churches, but nothing really worked for me. I started blogging with other people in my predicament and found that there is a market for certified kitchens that people can rent on an hourly basis to start their food businesses. In the summer of 2008, I took the plunge and left my IT job to open the kitchen and bake, and I haven't looked back.

What made you think there was a need for a kitchen incubator in your community?

Based on my experience and talking to quite a few others like myself online, I realized that there was a need for a kitchen incubator in the area. After opening, I have talked to many people who gush about how they have been looking for something like this for years and how happy they are to have found us.

How do most of your customers learn about your business/services?

Most people find us online through our Web site, Google searches, or other blogs, and we are starting to get a lot of word-of-mouth advertising through our satisfied customers.

Can you share what services participants will receive from your incubator?

We love to help people start food-based businesses. Navigating the legal requirements can be tricky, so we offer guidance through the entire process, from getting the necessary certifications and insurance to permits and inspections. We also have a list of vendors we have worked with that we refer clients to for raw ingredients, service items, etc. Also, we try to help our clients market themselves as much as possible. We have a monthly newsletter with leads in the area, such as trade shows, farmer's markets, and foodie dinners. Our Web site has a client listing that we offer free to our clients for advertising, as well as a community board in the kitchen and a referral service if the kitchen gets an inquiry about needing a specific item or service.

Can anyone open an incubator? What is needed to operate a kitchen incubator? (For example, prior business experience, working in food service, etc.)

It takes a lot of work to open an incubator. Most of the time, there is no other business like it in the area, and most people have never heard of the concept, so it seems like you are constantly reinventing the wheel. From permits to insurance to start-up capital, you are constantly explaining the business and how it will work (and that it will work). It takes a lot more work than opening a business that people are familiar with, like a fast-food franchise or a dry cleaners. It would definitely be helpful to have some business experience as well as a food background, as there are no best practices already tested that you can follow. Selling your ideas to investors and banks takes a lot of salesmanship and passion, so it is something you really have to want to do and believe in.

How do you determine what to charge clients?

We charge clients on an hourly basis, with discounts based on how much they use the facility per week. We do not have a minimum number of hours that clients have to use or a membership fee. It is all based on usage.

What does a client need to use the facility in the way of permits, licenses, insurance, etc.?

We have to follow all the health code requirements for our area, which include:

- At least one certified food manager per business
- Everyone else in the kitchen with that business must have a food handler's card

We then require everyone to have a general liability insurance policy, which covers the client as well as the kitchen in case of a foodborne illness. Clients also put down a security deposit before they can use the kitchen.

Once all of these items are in place, our clients can get a health/food or manufacturing permit from their governing health department, using us as their physical location for producing their food products.

What is most rewarding about operating a kitchen incubator?

The most rewarding aspect of the kitchen is seeing our clients build their businesses, and doing something they love at the same time. We recently had two clients who had their products picked up by local grocery and specialty stores, so it is great to walk in and see their products on the shelves.

What has been most challenging about operating a kitchen incubator?

Helping new businesses navigate the start-up process without losing their enthusiasm is challenging. When launching a new product, it can take up to two months before everything is in place for them to start producing and selling their product.

During the wait, it can be hard to keep their spirits up and be ready to go when everything is set.

What is in the future for Elixir Kitchen Space?

We hope to expand to other markets where we see the need for a kitchen incubator. After only being open for nine months, we can definitely see the need for kitchens in other cities, and I get calls and e-mails all the time from people asking when we will be in their city.

Appendix A
My Top Home Bakery Products

Most home-based bakers start out with a favorite family recipe or product idea in mind. It might be a pie, cake, cookie, scone, bar, or bread. Some recipes start from a simple idea created from a strong desire to think outside the box and come up with something that is not currently being sold in the local marketplace.

Remember, your kitchen is your laboratory; it is the place where you put your imagination to work and create products that will delight the public. Some of the best home-based bakery ideas come from existing recipes that have been tweaked. Even more dynamic recipes have come from mistakes, adding the wrong amount of some ingredient, resulting in a product that is unlike anything the baker could have anticipated.

The following are some of my favorite home-based bakery recipes that I have developed over the years in my own business. They have stood the test of time and are sure to please even the most discriminating palates. Feel free to give them a try in your own kitchen and to use them in your home-based bakery business.

Whipped Cream Biscuits
Yield: 8 to 10 large biscuits
These are the richest biscuits on the planet. Don't overmix. Serve them with a good homemade jam or jelly. You can also split the biscuit and fill it with a sausage patty, or a slice of grilled ham and shredded cheddar cheese. Once you taste these biscuits, your imagination is sure to fly sky high.

Ingredients
2 cups all-purpose flour

1 ½ tablespoons sugar

4 teaspoons baking powder

½ teaspoon cream of tartar

¼ teaspoon salt

½ cup (1 stick) unsalted butter, cut into small cubes

⅔ cup whipping cream, plus more as needed (do not substitute with anything else)

2 tablespoons melted butter

Directions

1. Preheat oven to 375 degrees.
2. Sift flour, sugar, baking powder, cream of tartar, and salt into medium bowl.
3. Cut in cubed butter until mixture resembles coarse meal.
4. Add cream and stir until just blended. The dough should be soft, yet firm enough to hold together. If you need a bit more cream, add it a teaspoon at a time.
5. Turn dough onto a lightly floured board/surface. Knead for 10 seconds. (If you handle the dough too much, the biscuits will be tough.)
6. Pat dough into a 1-inch-thick round.
7. Cut into 8 or 10 rounds using a 2-inch biscuit cutter.
8. Arrange biscuits on a large baking sheet, spacing them 1 inch apart. Bake until biscuits have risen and tops are lightly golden brown, about 15 minutes.
9. Transfer to cooling racks.
10. Brush the biscuit tops with melted butter, and serve hot or at room temperature.

Grandma's Sour Cream Pound Cake

Serves 8 to 10

There are hundreds of pound cake recipes, and everyone's mother, grandmother, aunt, uncle, and cousin has their own version. Pound cakes are tricky, but the best way to learn is to just jump right in. If you are using a Bundt pan, purchase a heavy-duty aluminum pan or a good tube pan; both will work well for this exceptional pound cake.

Ingredients

2 cups butter, softened

3 cups white sugar

6 eggs

1 teaspoon vanilla extract

1 teaspoon bourbon or rum

3 cups unbleached all-purpose flour

$\frac{1}{4}$ teaspoon baking soda

$\frac{1}{2}$ teaspoon salt

1 pinch ground mace

1 cup sour cream

1 tablespoon confectioners' sugar for dusting

Directions

1. Preheat the oven to 350 degrees. Grease and flour a 10-inch Bundt pan or 9-inch tube pan.
2. In a large bowl, cream together the butter and sugar until smooth; this may take 8 to 10 minutes. This is where a lot of bakers go wrong—the butter-sugar mixture should be fluffy and smooth; just when you think it won't get there, the structure changes and you have a cloud of buttery sweetness.
3. Beat in the eggs one at a time, mixing well after each, then stir in the vanilla.
4. In a separate bowl, combine the flour, baking soda, salt, and mace. Mix into the batter just until smooth.
5. Stir in sour cream and bourbon or rum.
6. Spoon batter into the prepared (greased and floured) pan, and spread evenly.
7. Bake for 1 hour and 20 minutes.
8. Cool for at least 10 minutes before inverting pan onto a plate, and tapping out the cake.
9. Dust with confectioners' sugar before serving.

Cream Sherry Bundt Cake

Serves 8 to 10

My cousin gave my mom this recipe, and although I rarely use cake mixes, you will understand why I do when you make this cake. You do not need to purchase expensive cream sherry, a bottle from the wine section at the grocery store will do fine; just make sure it is cream sherry. I once gave these cakes out to my staff at Christmas. Guess what? They expected them every Christmas after that!

Ingredients
1 package (18.25 ounces) yellow cake mix
4 eggs
3/4 cup vegetable oil
3/4 cup cream sherry
1 teaspoon ground nutmeg
1 package (3.5 ounces) instant vanilla pudding mix

Directions
1. Preheat oven to 350 degrees.
2. Grease the sides and bottom of a 10-inch Bundt cake pan. Flour the sides and bottom of the pan; tap out the excess flour.
3. In a large bowl, combine the cake mix, eggs, oil, sherry, nutmeg, and pudding mix. Beat until well blended. Pour the batter into the Bundt pan.
4. Bake for 45 minutes or until a toothpick inserted into the cake comes out clean. Cool in pan for 10 minutes, then turn out onto a wire rack.
5. While cake is still hot, glaze with Cream Sherry Glaze.

Cream Sherry Glaze
Yield: 1/2 cup
This glaze may be made ahead and reheated.

Ingredients
2 tablespoons butter, melted
3/4 cup powdered sugar
4 tablespoons cream sherry

Directions

1. In a medium pot add the butter, sugar, and sherry.
2. Whisk butter, sugar, and sherry together.
3. Put on low heat and stir until slightly thickened and reduced, approximately 8-10 minutes.
4. Glaze cake while it is still hot.

Banana & Maraschino Nut Loaf

Yield: 1 loaf (about 16 slices)

This is a wonderful little loaf I found in the *Detroit Free Press* in 1985. It has undergone a number of modifications, but it is wonderful with coffee or tea. If you have bananas that are too ripe, this is the bread to make.

Ingredients

1 jar (10-ounces) maraschino cherries

1 3/4 cups unbleached all-purpose flour

2 teaspoons baking powder

1/2 teaspoon salt

2/3 cup firmly packed light brown sugar

1/3 cup butter, softened

2 eggs

1/2 teaspoon vanilla extract

1 cup mashed ripe bananas (approximately 2 large bananas)

1/2 cup chopped walnuts

Directions

1. Preheat oven to 350 degrees.
2. Drain maraschino cherries, reserving 2 tablespoons juice.
3. Cut cherries into quarters; set aside.
4. Combine flour, baking powder, and salt in small bowl; set aside.
5. In medium bowl, combine brown sugar, butter, eggs, vanilla, and reserved cherry juice; mix at medium speed with an electric mixer until ingredients are thoroughly combined.
6. Alternate adding the flour mixture and the mashed bananas to the sugar mixture, beginning and ending with flour mixture.

7. Stir in cherries and nuts.
8. Lightly spray 9-inch x 5-inch x 3-inch loaf pan with nonstick cooking spray.
9. Spread batter evenly in pan.
10. Bake for 1 hour or until loaf is golden brown and wooden toothpick inserted near center comes out clean.
11. Remove from pan and cool on wire rack.
12. Store in tightly covered container or wrapped in foil.

Walnut Raisin Pumpkin Bread

Yield: 3 small (7 x 3-inch) loaves

This recipe dropped out of a used cookbook I purchased at the King's Bookstore in downtown Detroit.

Ingredients

3 1/4 cups all-purpose flour

3 cups sugar

2 teaspoons baking soda

1 1/2 teaspoons salt

1 teaspoon ground nutmeg

1 teaspoon ground cinnamon

2 cups solid pack pumpkin puree

2/3 cup water

1 cup canola oil

4 eggs

1/2 cup chopped walnuts (optional)

1/2 cup golden raisins (optional)

Directions

1. Preheat oven to 350 degrees.
2. Grease and flour three 7 x 3-inch bread pans.
3. Measure flour, sugar, baking soda, salt, and spices into a large bowl. Stir to blend.
4. Add pumpkin, water, canola oil, eggs, nuts, and raisins.
5. Beat until well combined.
6. Pour batter into prepared pans.
7. Bake for approximately 1 hour.

Best Brownies

Yield: 16 Brownies

This is a rich fudge brownie; just don't overbake it.

Ingredients

$^1\!/_2$ cup butter

1 cup sugar

2 eggs

1 teaspoon vanilla extract

$^1\!/_3$ cup unsweetened cocoa powder

$^1\!/_2$ cup all-purpose flour

$^1\!/_4$ teaspoon salt

$^1\!/_4$ teaspoon baking powder

1 cup white chocolate morsels (optional)

Directions

1. Preheat oven to 350 degrees.
2. Grease and flour an 8-inch square pan.
3. In a large saucepan, melt $^1\!/_2$ cup butter.
4. Remove from heat, and stir in sugar, eggs, and vanilla.
5. Beat in cocoa, flour, salt, and baking powder.
6. Spread batter into prepared pan.
7. Sprinkle with white chocolate morsels.
8. Bake for 25 to 30 minutes. Do not overbake.

Down-Home Dinner Rolls

Yield: about 18 rolls

This recipe has few ingredients but yields rolls that are absolutely delicious. They also reheat beautifully.

Ingredients

About 7 cups unbleached all-purpose flour

6 tablespoons plus $^1\!/_4$ teaspoon sugar

1 $^1\!/_4$ teaspoon salt

3 packages dry yeast

2 ¼ cups hot water (105 to 115 degrees Fahrenheit)

⅓ cup canola or vegetable oil (do not use olive oil)

5 tablespoons butter, melted

Directions

1. In a large bowl, mix 6 cups of the flour, 6 tablespoons of the sugar, and the salt.
2. In a separate bowl, combine the yeast and the hot water.
3. Sprinkle in about ¼ teaspoon sugar over the yeast-water mixture. Cover with a piece of plastic wrap.
4. Let sit for 5 to 10 minutes; stir briefly, the yeast will start to bubble and grow.
5. Add the oil to the liquid mixture. Stir gently and set aside.
6. Make a well in the middle of the flour mixture, and add half the liquid mixture.
7. Mix with a wooden spoon; as the liquid is incorporated, add more liquid.
8. When the mixture cannot be stirred by the spoon, use your hands to knead in the remaining cup of flour. (If the dough is still too dry, add 1 or 2 table-spoons of warm water.)
9. Pour the dough out onto a floured surface and slowly incorporate any remaining flour. You may not use the entire 7 cups, but then again you may. The dough should be soft and pliable.
10. Knead for about 10 minutes . . . take your time. If you get tired, stop. Let the dough rest for 2 minutes, then continue.
11. Smooth the dough into a ball and place in a greased bowl to rise.
12. Remember to turn the dough once so both sides are greased.
13. Cover the dough with plastic wrap to seal it tightly. Place in a warm spot (e.g., over the clothes dryer if it is running) for about 40 minutes.
14. The dough may rise to the top of the plastic. After rising, punch down the dough and form into balls.
15. Place 2- to 2 ½-inch balls into a greased 9-inch x 12-inch x 3-inch pan.
16. Cover with a dry, clean towel and once again place on top of clothes dryer or any other warm spot for 20 to 25 minutes for the second rise.

17. Preheat oven to 350 degrees. Brush rolls with melted butter (about 3 to 4 tablespoons), and bake on middle rack for 16 to 22 minutes until golden brown.
18. After rolls are done, brush with any leftover butter and serve.

Basic Dog Treat Recipe

Yield: 48 treats

I once made these dog treats as a gift for my neighbor, and all I can say is they went over well!

Ingredients

1 cup rolled oats

¼ cup margarine

1 cup boiling water

1 cup cornmeal

3 teaspoons sugar

½ cup beef broth

¼ cup skim milk

1 ½ cup shredded cheddar cheese

1 egg, beaten

3 cups whole wheat flour

Directions

1. Preheat oven to 325 degrees. Grease cookie sheets.
2. In a large bowl, combine the oats, margarine, and boiling water. Let stand 15 minutes.
3. Stir cornmeal, sugar, beef broth, and milk into the oat mixture. Add cheddar cheese and egg.
4. Mix in flour, 1 cup at a time, to form a stiff dough.
5. Knead dough on a lightly floured surface, mixing in additional flour as needed until the dough is smooth and no longer sticky.
6. Roll or pat out dough to ½-inch thickness
7. Cut with dog bone cookie cutters and place 1-inch apart on the greased cookie sheets.

8. Bake 35 to 45 minutes, until golden. Dog treats should be crisp.
9. Cool completely before storing in a loosely covered container or plastic bag.

The following recipes were selected from my family cookbook *Little Black Book of Pies*, which is no longer in print. Enjoy!

Three Old Time Pie Crust Recipes

Crust #1

Yield: 2 9-inch pie crusts

This is one of the first pie crust recipes I learned more than twenty-five years ago. I have since experimented with a number of recipes, but this one is tried and true. I sometimes use the butter-flavored Crisco, depending on the filling, but you decide what your taste buds like best.

Ingredients

2 ¹/₂ cups sifted all-purpose flour
¹/₂ teaspoon salt
³/₄ cup solid vegetable shortening (Crisco)
6 to 7 tablespoons ice water

Directions

1. Sift together the flour and salt.
2. Add ¹/₂ cup of the shortening to the flour mixture using a pastry stir or fork to cut the shortening into the flour until the mixture has the texture of cornmeal.
3. Add the remaining shortening, and cut in until the mixture is the size of small peas.
4. Add the water, 1 tablespoon at a time, while tossing the mixture with a fork. Add only enough water to make the dough stick together.
5. Press the dough into a ball, and cut the ball in half.
6. Wrap each half in waxed paper, and chill until ready to use.
7. On a lightly floured surface roll out each half to about ¹/₈ inch thick.
8. Gently place the dough in a greased and floured 9-inch round pie pan. Press to fit the sides and bottom. Trim edges.
9. Refrigerate 20 minutes before filling.

Crust #2

Yield: 1 9-inch pie crust

For those times when you just need one pie crust.

Ingredients

1 ½ cups all-purpose flour

¼ teaspoon salt

½ cup solid vegetable shortening (Crisco)

2 to 3 tablespoons ice water

Directions

1. Sift together the flour and salt.
2. Add the shortening, using a pastry stir or fork to cut in the shortening until the mixture has the texture of cornmeal.
3. Add the water, 1 tablespoon at a time, while tossing the mixture with a fork. Add only enough water to make the dough stick together.
4. Press the dough into a ball.
5. Wrap in waxed paper and chill until ready to use.
6. On a lightly floured surface, roll out dough to about ⅛ inch thick.
7. Gently place the dough in a greased and floured 9-inch round pie pan. Press to fit the sides and bottom. Trim edges.
8. Refrigerate 20 minutes before filling.

Crust #3

Yield: 1 8-inch pie crust

Sweet pie crusts are not needed often, but when you want something a bit different, try this recipe. It is perfect for heavy fillings like pumpkin, sweet potato, and Irish potato pie.

Ingredients

3 tablespoons unsalted butter, softened

2 tablespoons granulated sugar

¼ teaspoon salt

1 small egg, beaten

2 tablespoons cold milk (whole milk or 2 percent only)

1 cup plus 2 tablespoons all-purpose flour

Directions

1. Place the softened butter, sugar, and salt in a mixing bowl. Using an electric mixer, beat on high speed until mixture is creamy.
2. Add the egg and beat 25 seconds.
3. Add the milk and beat on high speed for 1 1/2 minutes.
4. Add the 1 cup plus 2 tablespoons of all-purpose flour and beat the dough for 5 to 7 more seconds. The dough will be soft.
5. Form into a ball and wrap in plastic wrap; refrigerate for at least 1 hour.
6. Roll out on lightly floured surface until 1/8 inch thick.
7. Gently place the dough in a greased and floured 8-inch round pie pan. Press to fit the sides and bottom. Trim edges.
8. Refrigerate 20 minutes before filling.

Whole Wheat Pie Crust

Yield: 2 9-inch pie crusts

This is one of my favorite whole wheat pie crust recipes. It is simple and delicious and perfect for sweet or savory pies.

Ingredients

2 1/2 cups whole wheat pastry flour

1/2 teaspoon salt

3/4 cup cold butter, diced

1/2 cup cold milk (whole)—Keep the milk cold by putting the cup of milk in a container filled with ice. The key to a flaky crust is to keep the ingredients cold.

Directions

1. Combine flour and salt in mixing bowl.
2. Work quickly and toss in cold butter and combine using a fork. Mix thoroughly so butter is evenly distributed.
3. Add the cold milk a tablespoon at a time; you may need it all, you may not. Add just enough to hold the dough together. The dough should still be a bit loose and dry, not wet and sticky.

4. Form the dough into two balls and wrap in wax paper.
5. Chill until ready to use.
6. Roll out the two balls of dough between two sheets of floured waxed paper until ⅛ inch thick.
7. Fit into pie shell and use as directed in recipe

Pie Crust for Fruit Pies

Yield: 1 9-inch pie crust (bottom and lattice top)

I am not particularly fond of sweet pie dough, but this recipe is really perfect for most fruit pies. The crust is a bit rich and heavier than most. It is almost cookie-like. The addition of egg yolk gives it a rich flavor that most crusts lack. I personally like this pie crust for fresh peach pie (canned peaches do not do it justice).

Ingredients

2 cups flour

2 tablespoons confectioners' sugar

1 ½ teaspoons granulated sugar

½ teaspoon salt

10 tablespoons butter

1 egg yolk, beaten

1 ½ tablespoons water

Milk, heavy cream, or egg white (for brushing on top)

Directions

1. Sift all dry ingredients in mixing bowl.
2. Cut butter into dry mixture with pastry blender or fork. Handle mixture quickly.
3. Add the beaten egg yolk and water.
4. Shape into a ball.
5. Wrap in waxed paper and refrigerate for 1 hour.
6. Roll out on a lightly floured surface until ⅛ inch thick.
7. Cut out base of pie bottom.
8. Use remaining dough to make lattice top.
9. Brush lattice top with milk, heavy cream, or egg white; do not brush the edges. I, personally, prefer heavy cream, but try using milk and see how

you like it; the next time you bake a pie, use egg white. The preference you select will be passed down as your culinary legacy.

Old Fashioned Pie Crust Using Lard

Yield: 2 9-inch pie crusts

This is an old-fashioned pie crust recipe with four simple ingredients. It is shocking how so little can come together and taste so good. I was always told that lard makes the best pie crust, and it is true, it really does.

Ingredients

2 ½ cups all-purpose flour

1 teaspoon salt

¾ cup lard

⅓ cup ice water

Directions

1. Sift flour and salt into a mixing bowl.
2. Cut lard into the mixture using a pastry stir or fork until it looks like course meal.
3. Add ice water, 1 tablespoon at a time.
4. Gather dough into one large ball, then divide in half (careful, don't over-work the dough).
5. Wrap each ball of dough in waxed paper and chill for 1 hour.
6. Roll out each half on a lightly floured surface until ⅛ inch thick.
7. Use as directed in pie recipe.

Old-Fashioned Hot Water Pie Crust

Yield: 2 9-inch pie crusts

This recipe is the first hot water pie crust I learned to make. I have since modified the recipe to include milk. This is a flaky, tasty pie crust.

Ingredients

1 cup minus 2 tablespoons shortening, melted

¼ cup hot water

1 tablespoon whole milk (you can substitute 2 percent but nothing less)

2 ¼ cups all purpose flour
½ teaspoon salt

Directions
1. Place shortening in large bowl. Pour hot water and milk over it.
2. With a dinner fork, break up the shortening.
3. Tilt bowl and beat quickly until the mixture looks murky and creamy.
4. Pour flour and salt over shortening mixture. Beat well with a fork, forming a dough.
5. Divide into two parts and roll out between two sheets of floured waxed paper.
6. Fit into pie shell and use as directed in recipe.

Variations:
Cheddar Cheese Pastry Shell—Stir in ½ cup finely grated cheddar cheese with the shortening.
Nice and Nutty Pastry Shell—Add ½ cup ground walnuts or pecans to flour-shortening mixture before adding hot water.

Christmas Cranberry Crunch Pie
Yield: 1 9-inch deep-dish pie
I am a big fan of all things cranberry, but everyone is not, so this unusual pie may be a bit tart for some. The pie sort of makes its own crust, and the crunch of the walnuts marries beautifully with vanilla ice cream. Serve this pie slightly warm with vanilla ice cream.

Ingredients
2 cups whole fresh cranberries, rinsed
1 ½ cups sugar
½ cup light brown sugar, firmly packed
½ cup walnuts, coarsely chopped
2 eggs, beaten
½ teaspoon vanilla extract
1 cup sifted all purpose flour

1 1/4 teaspoons baking powder

3/4 cup unsalted butter, melted

Directions

1. Preheat oven to 325 degrees.
2. Thoroughly grease the bottom and sides of a 9-inch deep-dish pie pan/plate.
3. Spread the washed fresh cranberries in the buttered pie pan.
4. Combine 1/2 cup sugar, light brown sugar, and walnuts; set aside.
5. Sprinkle half of the sugar/walnut mixture over the cranberries.
6. Mix the remaining sugar with the eggs and vanilla; beat thoroughly.
7. Mix in flour and baking powder.
8. Stir in melted butter.
9. Pour the batter over the cranberries and top with the remaining sugar/walnut mixture.
10. Bake for about 1 hour or until golden brown.

Old-Fashioned Chess Lemon Pie

Yield: 1 9-inch pie

This is another family favorite. It is a tart and rich pie; a gift from my cousin. Just serve it at room temperature with a hot cup of coffee. This is the kind of pie folks will remember for days and days.

Ingredients

4 eggs

1 1/4 cups granulated sugar

7 tablespoons butter, melted

1 level tablespoon all-purpose flour

4 tablespoons fresh lemon juice

1 tablespoon finely grated lemon peel

1/8 teaspoon vanilla extract

Pinch salt

Directions

1. Preheat oven to 350 degrees.

2. Beat eggs well.
3. Add sugar, butter, and flour, beating well after each addition. Mixture should be smooth and silky. Check mixture for lumps of flour.
4. Stir in vanilla, lemon juice, grated lemon peel, and salt.
5. Pour into unbaked pie shell.
6. Bake until set, 35 to 40 minutes, or until a knife inserted near center comes out clean.
7. If the top begins to brown too quickly, cover pie with aluminum foil tent.

Old-Fashioned Southern Pecan Pie

Yield: 1 9-inch pie

I have always loved pecan pie, and this is an exceptional recipe. It looks simple, and it is; I simply suggest you use a really good vanilla extract. If you don't want to purchase Ronald Reginald Vanilla, use one with an exceptional flavor that will mix well with the pecans. Do not overbake this pie, and remember to always serve it slightly warm or at room temperature. Yes, refrigerate leftovers, but serve them at room temperature, too.

Ingredients
²/₃ cup plus 1 tablespoon granulated sugar
³/₄ cup light corn syrup
4 eggs, beaten
2 tablespoons melted butter
1 teaspoon vanilla extract
Pinch salt
1 cup pecans, chopped

Directions
1. Preheat oven to 350 degrees.
2. In large bowl, combine sugar, corn syrup, eggs, melted butter, vanilla, salt, and pecans.
3. Mix well. Pour into unbaked pie shell.
4. Bake for 45 minutes, checking after 35 minutes to see if crust is browning too quickly. If it is, cover with aluminum foil.

5. Allow pie to bake remainder of time or until a knife inserted in center comes out clean (do not overbake).
6. Cool completely, waiting at least 1 hour before serving.

October's Pumpkin Pie

Yield: 1 9-inch pie

I love a rich, light, silky pumpkin pie, and this is the one. Serve it at room temperature with vanilla ice cream or sweetened whipped cream.

Ingredients

1 cup light brown sugar, firmly packed

4 tablespoons all-purpose flour

1 teaspoon ground cinnamon

$1/4$ teaspoon ground cloves

$1/4$ teaspoon ground nutmeg

$1/2$ teaspoon ground ginger

$1/2$ teaspoon salt

2 egg yolks, beaten

1 cup milk

$1/4$ cup butter, melted

2 egg whites, whipped to soft peaks

1 cup canned pumpkin puree

Directions

1. Preheat oven to 350 degrees.
2. In a mixing bowl combine the sugar, flour, spices, and salt.
3. In the top of a double boiler set over simmering water, combine the egg yolks and milk.
4. Stir in the sugar mixture and butter, gently stir until slightly thick.
5. Remove mixture from heat and set aside to cool for 20 minutes.
6. Add 1 cup canned pumpkin puree to cooled egg-milk mixture.
7. Fold in beaten egg whites.
8. Gently turn pumpkin mixture into into pie shell.
9. Bake for 20 to 25 minutes or until knife inserted in center comes out clean.

Auntee's Oatmeal Pie

Yield: 1 9-inch pie

My great-aunt once had this pie at a cafeteria restaurant in either Texas or Louisiana. She asked for the recipe and got it. I would eat this pie for breakfast, lunch, or dinner. Serve at room temperature.

Ingredients

1/2 cup light brown sugar

1/2 cup granulated sugar

1/2 cup butter, melted

3/4 cup quick cooking oats

1/2 cup flaked coconut

1 cup whole milk

3/4 cup dark corn syrup

2 eggs, lightly beaten

1 teaspoon vanilla extract

1/2 cup chopped walnuts

Directions

1. Preheat oven to 350 degrees.
2. Combine all ingredients in a mixing bowl and stir until smooth.
3. Pour mixture into an unbaked deep dish pie shell.
4. Bake for 35 to 45 minutes, until knife inserted in center comes out clean.

Sweet Bean Pie

Yield: 1 9-inch pie

This is an unusual, dense, sweet, tasty pie reminiscent of sweet potato pie. Truly economical, this pie is made with navy beans. It has a unique, creamy, addictive taste and is the perfect ending to any meal. Serve at room temperature.

Ingredients

2 cups dried navy beans (do not use canned)

2 eggs, beaten

1 cup evaporated milk

2/3 cup plus 1 tablespoon granulated sugar

$^1\!/_2$ teaspoon salt

$^3\!/_4$ teaspoon ground cinnamon

$^1\!/_2$ teaspoon ground nutmeg

$^1\!/_2$ teaspoon ground cloves

1 egg white, whipped to soft peaks

Directions

1. Place 2 cups dried navy beans in 4 cups of water on medium heat until beans are soft and tender, about 2 or more hours.
2. Cool, drain, and puree in food processor with 3 tablespoons of water from cooked beans.
3. Measure 2 cups of cooked pureed beans for this recipe; mixture will be thick and stiff.
4. Preheat oven to 425 degrees.
5. In a large bowl, combine eggs, evaporated milk, and mashed navy beans. Mix well.
6. Add sugar, salt, cinnamon, ginger, nutmeg, and cloves. Mix until all ingredients are thoroughly combined (mixture should be creamy).
7. Fold in egg white.
8. Pour mixture into unbaked pastry shells.
9. Bake for 15 minutes.
10. Reduce heat to 350 degrees and bake an additional 35 minutes.

Pineapple Brule Pie

Yield: 1 9-inch pie

My mother originally made this pie without the Brule topping. Many years ago I added the topping when I made it for radio talk show host Joy Taylor-Skiba on WEXL AM-Radio in Royal Oak, Michigan. If you like pineapple, you will love this pie. It is not too sweet, with a hint of crunch. You just have to taste it to believe it. It is wonderful!

Ingredients

7 tablespoons butter, melted

1 $^1\!/_4$ cup granulated sugar

3 eggs

1 teaspoon vanilla extract

1 teaspoon all-purpose flour

1 can (8 ½ ounces) crushed pineapple, drained, with liquid reserved

Directions

1. Preheat oven to 350 degrees.
2. Combine butter, sugar, eggs, vanilla, and flour. Stir until smooth.
3. Stir in crushed pineapple and 1 tablespoon of reserved pineapple liquid.
4. Pour filling into pie shell.
5. Bake for 35 minutes.
6. Carefully remove pie from oven. Sprinkle Sweet Cinnamon Crumb topping on pie and continue baking another 10 to 12 minutes until topping is brown.
7. Allow pie to cool before serving.

Sweet Cinnamon Crumb Topping

Yield: about 2 cups

There will be times when a top pastry shell is not needed. You just want something crumbly and sweet. This crumb topping is great on any fruit pie—cherry, Concord grape, apple, fig, or peach. My grandmother, Mama Lula, had a fig tree in her yard in Clinton, Louisiana, and she loved to put up fig preserves. If you are lucky enough to have access to fresh figs, a fig pie with this topping will have the church ladies talking. This crumb mixture can be made ahead and stored in the refrigerator in a sealed container.

Ingredients

1 cup plus 1 tablespoon all-purpose flour

⅓ cup granulated sugar

¼ cup light brown sugar, firmly packed

¼ teaspoon salt

½ teaspoon ground cinnamon

¼ pound (2 sticks) ice cold butter, grated, set aside in a bowl

Directions

1. Combine all ingredients in a bowl.
2. Mix on low with electric mixer (hand-held is adequate).
3. Rub the mixture with your fingers to create big crumbs.

4. Sprinkle evenly over the top of pie, cover all of the fruit.
5. Bake according to pie directions.
6. Top will brown and crisp, and any juices will bubble through.

Weights, Measures and Conversions

(Retrieved from the United States Department of Agriculture Nutrient Data Laboratory www.nal
.usda.gov/fnic/foodcomp/Bulletins/measurement_equivalents.html)

Measurement Equivalents for Kitchen Use
1 tablespoon = 3 teaspoons
2 tablespoons = 1 fluid ounce
4 tablespoons = ¼ cup or 2 ounces
5 ⅓ tablespoons = ⅓ cup or 2 ⅔ ounces
8 tablespoons = ½ cup or 4 ounces
16 tablespoons = 1 cup or 8 ounces
¼ cup = 4 tablespoons
⅓ cup = 5 tablespoons plus 1 teaspoon
½ cup = 8 tablespoons
⅔ cup =10 tablespoons plus 2 teaspoons
¾ cup = 12 tablespoons
1 cup = 48 teaspoons or ½ pint or 8 fluid ounces
2 cups = 1 pint or 16 fluid ounces
1 pint, liquid = 16 fluid ounces
1 quart, liquid = 2 pints or 4 cups
1 gallon, liquid = 4 quarts

Appendix B
Resources

The following programs, business books, software, videos, and online resources can help you get your home-based business started:

Culinary Schools/Pastry Programs

There are many patisserie and baking programs where home-based bakers can fine-tune their skills and even pick up a certificate, an associates, or a bachelors degree in the culinary field. If that is your desire, you might consider some of the programs listed below:

The Culinary Institute of America at Greystone
2555 Main Street
St. Helena, CA 94574
 (800)-CULINARY
www.ciachef.edu/
The Culinary Institute of America at Greystone offers a thirty-week Associate in Occupational Studies (A.O.S.) degree program in baking and pastry arts.

Johnson & Wales University
Culinary Arts Division
801 West Trade Street
Charlotte, NC 28202
www.jwu.edu
Johnson & Wales University has a most prestigious two-year Baking & Pastry Arts associate degree program that will teach students about classical French pastries, artisan breads, wedding cakes, plated desserts, and the creation of masterful showpieces.

Le Cordon Bleu Schools of North America

Patisserie and Baking Programs & Degrees

1927 Lakeside Parkway

Tucker, GA 30084

(888) 675-5222

www.chefs.edu/ for program locations

The Le Cordon Bleu Schools of North America offer a thirty-six-week program in Patisserie and Baking. It includes thirty weeks on campus followed by a six-week internship.

Home-based bakers may also want to contact their local community colleges or adult education/lifelong learning curriculums to see if they have culinary programs that offer bakery and/or pastry courses. These programs and courses are sometimes less expensive and offer more flexibility. You may also want to check local bakeries in your area and see if the owners are offering professional classes.

Suggested Workshops and Seminars

There are several community centers, private bakery and pastry shops, as well as numerous craft stores that offer workshops for home bakers.

Culinary School for the Rockies—Boulder, Colorado

www.culinaryschoolrockies.com

The school offers workshops in cooking and pastry for the home cook, along with basic baking and pastry techniques.

The French Pastry School—Chicago, Illinois

www.frenchpastryschool.com/index.html

The classes offered by The French Pastry School do not require experience in pastry or bread baking and their students come from diverse backgrounds. The goal of the instruction is to tap students' raw talent and develop their baking skills.

San Francisco Baking Institute—San Francisco, California

www.sfbi.com/workshops.html

The workshops are limited to sixteen students and cater to both professional and home-based bakers who want to take their love of baking to the next level.

The Wilton School of Cake Decorating and Confectionary Art

7511 Lemont Road

Darien, IL 60561

(800) 772-7111 ext. 2888

www.wilton.com

The Wilton Company has been teaching cake decoration classes since 1929, when Dewey McKinley Wilton opened a cake-decorating and candy-making school for caterers and chefs in his Chicago home. Today Wilton offers a wide variety of classes for bakers at every level.

Videos

Many home-based bakers do not have time to take professional baking classes at a culinary arts school. Listed here are a couple of professional baking DVDs that can help you improve your baking skills.

About Professional Baking DVD Series, Delmar Learning, (CENGAGE Delmar Learning, 2008).

The Best of America's Test Kitchen: Best Baking Recipes, (WGBH Boston, PBS, 2008).

Software

Cake pricing matrixes help cake makers figure a total cost for a cake, including time, overhead, and delivery. Matrixes can come in a number of forms. It might be a CD-ROM or a simple Excel spreadsheet. There is currently only one program to my knowledge, offered by the CakeBoss. It helps calculate the exact cost of a cake and can be purchased online from www.cakeboss.com.

Online Resources

The following Web sites can assist you in troubleshooting issues with specific recipes. You can also find online discussion forums for locating specific bakery products and supplies:

Online Baking Resources

America's Test Kitchens: www.americastestkitchentv.com

BakingBuyer.com: www.bakingbuyer.com

Cake Central: http://cakecentral.com

Cookinglight.com: www.cookinglight.com

Epicurious: www.epicurious.com

Food Network: www.foodnetwork.com

Joy of Baking: www.joyofbaking.com

King Arthur Free Online Baking Classes: www.kingarthurflour.com

Mixing Bowl: www.mixingbowl.com/home

Sugarcraft: www.sugarcraft.com

The Fresh Loaf: www.thefreshloaf.com

Very Best Baking: www.verybestbaking.com/advice/baking101/default.aspx

White Lily Flour Videos: www.whitelily.com/BakingTips/Tips_Video.aspx

Recommended Bakery Blogs

Bakerella: www.bakerella.com

Baking Bites: www.bakingbites.com

Baking Obsession: www.bakingobsession.com

Building a Bakery: http://buildingabakery.blogspot.com

Cupcake Project: www.cupcakeproject.com

Cupcakes Take the Cake: http://cupcakestakethecake.blogspot.com

David Lebovitz: www.davidlebovitz.com

Dessert First: http://dessertfirst.typepad.com

Dorie Greenspan: www.doriegreenspan.com

Engineer Baker: http://engineerbaker.blogspot.com

Gluten Free Girl: www.glutenfreegirl.blogspot.com

Joy the Baker: www.joythebaker.com

Orangette: www.orangette.blogspot.com

Spoonful: www.spoonfulblog.com

Tartelette: www.mytartelette.com

Books for the Home-Based Baker

Baker's Manual, Nicole Rees (John Wiley and Sons, Inc. 2003).

The Baker's Trade: A Recipe for Creating the Successful Small Bakery, Zachary Y. Schat (Action Circle Publishing Co., 1998).

Baking in America: Traditional and Contemporary Favorites from the Past 200 Years, Greg Patent (Houghton Mifflin Company, 2002).

Baking with Julia, Dorie Greenspan (William Morrow and Company, 1996).

Basic Baking: Everything You Need to Know to Start Baking Plus 101 Luscious Dessert Recipes that Anyone Can Make, Lora Brody (William Morrow and Company, 2000).

The Bread Baker's Apprentice: Mastering the Art of Bread, Peter Reinhart and Ron Manville (Ten Speed Press, 2001).

The Buttercup Bake Shop Cookbook, Jennifer Appel (Simon and Schuster, 2001).

The Cake Bible, Rose Levy Beranbaum (Morrow, 1988).

Confections of a Closet Master Baker: One Woman's Sweet Journey from Unhappy Hollywood Executive to Contented Country Baker, Gesine Bullock-Prado (Broadway Books, 2009).

Duct Tape Marketing: The World's Most Practical Small Business Marketing Guide, John Jantsch (Thomas Nelson, 2006).

From Kitchen to Market: Selling Your Gourmet Food Specialty, Stephen F. Hall (Dearborn Trade Publishing, 2005).

How Baking Works: Exploring the Fundamentals of Baking Science, Paula I. Figoni (John Wiley & Sons, Inc., 2008).

How to Open a Financially Successful Bakery: With a Companion CD-ROM, Sharon Fullen and Douglas R. Brown (Atlantic Publishing Group, Inc., 2004).

How to Succeed as a Small Business Owner and Still Have a Life, Bill Collier (Porchester Press, 2006).

The Pie and Pastry Bible, Rose Levy Beranbaum (Scribner, 1998).

The Secrets of Baking: Simple Techniques for Sophisticated Desserts, Sherry Yard (Houghton Mifflin Co., 2003).

The Simple Art of Perfect Baking, Flo Braker, (Chronicle Books, 2003).

Small Business Start-Up Kit, Peri Pakroo (NOLO, 2008).

Industry Magazines

American Cake Decorating Magazine
www.americancakedecorating.com/abt/acd_history.php

Bon Appetit
www.bonappetit.com/

Dessert Professionals
www.dessertprofessional.com/

Cook's Illustrated
www.cooksillustrated.com/

Fine Cooking
www.finecooking.com/

Gastronomica
www.gastronomica.org/

Gourmet
www.gourmet.com/

Martha Stewart Living
www.marthastewart.com/

Modern Baking
http://modern-baking.com/

Saveur
www.saveur.com/

Southern Living
www.southernliving.com/

Professional Organizations

American Culinary Federation
www.acfchefs.org//AM/Template.cfm?Section=Home6

International Association of Culinary Professionals
www.iacp.com/

Home Baking Association
www.homebaking.org/index.html

Sugar—Sweet by Nature
www.sugar.org/

The Bread Bakers Guild of America
www.bbga.org/

The James Beard Foundation
www.JamesBeard.org

Index

checklists. *See also* forms
  compliance, 47
  kitchen incubator, 22
  recipe development, 108
  Web site development, 120–21
checks, from customers, 131
Chess Lemon Pie, Old-Fashioned, 161–62
children
  caring for, 101–2
  as kitchen helpers, 15–16, 18
Chocolate Chip Butter Cookies, 111–12
Christmas Cranberry Crunch Pie, 160–61
cinnamon, 28–29
Cinnamon Crumb Topping, Sweet, 166–67
cleaners, household, 68
cloves, 29
commercial bakeries
  opposition to home-based bakeries, 1
  risks of, 2
company overview, in e-marketing plans, 85
competitors, 127–32
  developing edge over, 128, 130–31
  identifying, 127–28
  packaging and delivery, 129
  paying attention to, 128
  pricing, 76–77, 128–29
  social networking, 131–32
completed operations insurance, 42
compliance checklist, 47
compliance officers, 8
computers, 45
confidence, 70
contact information, on Web site, 130
contracts, 7, 21, 110, 136
conversions, 167
cookies
  Best Brownies, 152
  Chocolate Chip Butter Cookies, 111–12
  frosting, 33–34, 125, 138
  interview with baker of, 138–40
  Peanut Butter Cookies, 65
  shipping, 33–34, 125–26, 138
Cooking with Denay (Web site), 104
cookware, 25
copyright, 114
cost management, 14, 102
cottage food laws, 16–17, 56–57
Cranberry Crunch Pie, Christmas, 160–61
Cream Sherry Bundt Cake, 148–50
Cream Sherry Glaze, 149–50

credit cards, 119, 131
Crumb Topping, Sweet Cinnamon, 166–67
culinary schools/pastry programs, 168–69
curry powder, 29
customers
  baking at their homes, 109
  coming to your home, 135, 139
  contact procedures, 64
  identifying, 7
  keeping track of, 92–93
  number of potential, 1
  older, 80
  product ideas from, 112
  relations with, 39
  samples for, 3
customer service page, on Web site, 130

D
delivering products, 6–7, 59, 129
demographics, 80, 86
Dinner Rolls, Down-Home, 152–54
direct sales, 7
dishwashing, 19
dog treat company, 132, 141–42
Dog Treat Recipe, Basic, 154–55
domain names, 119
dry goods, basic, 28

E
e-commerce payment services, 93
e-commerce software, 119
egg white, raw, 33–34
Elixir Kitchen Space, 142–45
e-mail marketing services, 92
e-marketing plans, 84–86
equipment and supplies, basic cooking, 25–27
ethics, 38–39
extracts, 28

F
Facebook, 91, 132
family helpers, 15–16, 18
FAQs, on Web site, 130
farmer's markets, 38, 56, 129
fear, 114–15
federal taxes, 98–99
financial analysis, 49, 53

V
vanilla beans, 29
variable costs, 102
vehicle mileage documentation, 96
VeriSign, 123
videos, recommended, 170

W
Walnut Raisin Pumpkin Bread, 151
water source, 18, 57
Web sites. *See also* Internet; online sales
   business plan information on, 48
   checklist for developing, 120–21
   developing, 118–22
   food recall, 44
   food safety, 68
   importance of, 135
   message boards, baking, 77
   online selling, 130
   resources, general, 10, 104, 170–71
   social networking, 91, 104
weights, measures and conversions, 167
Whipped Cream Biscuits, 146–47
wholesale *vs.* retail production, 7, 73–74
Whole Wheat Pie Crust, 157–58
Willis, Diane, 132, 141–42
word-of-mouth advertising, 78, 90, 137
workers' compensation insurance, 42–43
work hours, 4, 6
worksheet, start-up cost, 14
workshops and seminars, 104, 169–70

Y
Yummy to Your Tummy, Desserts by Andrea, 91

Z
zoning, 42, 59

About the Author

Detra Denay Davis is from Detroit, Michigan. Her career journey has included working as a cook, food stylist, and caterer. Denay has been a home baker and all-around food enthusiast for more than twenty-five years. In 2008 Denay designed and taught a popular Lifelong Learning course for adults titled "How to Operate a Home-Based Bakery." Today she lives in Atlanta, Georgia, where she works as a consultant and online instructor working with food entrepreneurs nationwide.